Athlone French Poets

RIMBAUD

Athlone French Poets

General Editor EILEEN LE BRETON

This series is designed to provide students and general readers both with Monographs on important nineteenth- and twentieth-century French poets and Critical Editions of one or more representative works by these poets.

The Monographs aim at presenting the essential biographical facts while placing the poet in his social and intellectual context. They contain a detailed analysis of his poetical works and, where appropriate, a brief account of his other writings. His literary reputation is examined and his contribution to the development of French poetry is assessed, as is also his impact on other literatures. A selection of critical views and a bibliography are appended.

The critical Editions contain a substantial introduction aimed at presenting each work against its historical background as well as studying its genre, structure, themes, style, etc. and highlighting its relevance for today. The text normally given is the complete text of the original edition. It is followed by full commentaries on poems and annotation of the text, including variant readings when these are of real significance.

E. Le B.

RIMBAUD

by

C. CHADWICK

UNIVERSITY OF LONDON
THE ATHLONE PRESS
1979

Published by
THE ATHLONE PRESS
UNIVERSITY OF LONDON
at 4 Gower Street, London wc1

Distributed by
Tiptree Book Services Ltd
Tiptree, Essex

U.S.A. and Canada
Humanities Press Inc
New Jersey

British Library Cataloguing in Publications Data
Chadwick, Charles
Rimbaud.—(Athlone French Poets).
1. Rimbaud, Arthur—Criticism and interpretation
841'.8   PQ2387.R5Z/

ISBN 0 485 14610 x cloth
ISBN 0 485 12210 3 paperback

Printed in Great Britain by
Western Printing Services Limited
Bristol

PREFACE

Arthur Rimbaud has been subjected to a wider variety of attempts to explain his work than perhaps any other writer. Claudel saw him as a mystic unknowingly in search of God. The Surrealists emphasized the extent to which he could be considered as an explorer of the irrational and as a rebel against bourgeois concepts of order and meaning in art. Later critics, while laying equal emphasis on the transcendental aspect of Rimbaud's work, saw it neither in Christian nor in Surrealist terms but as an attempt to retain a childhood vision of the world, or as a further stage in the long history of the poet as a seer, or even as evidence of an interest in occultism and alchemy. One or two more recent commentators, reacting against what they see as a tendency to exaggerate the metaphysical aspect of Rimbaud's writings, have emphasized the extent to which the *Illuminations* in particular seem to them to be more firmly founded in reality than has usually been supposed.

These and other interpretations are, however, perhaps less widely different from one another than they may seem. There is general agreement that Rimbaud shared the tendency, common among poets of the late nineteenth century, to turn away from reality towards another world, even if there is some dispute as to why he wished to do so, where the frontier between the two should be drawn, what means he used to achieve his goal, and how that goal is to be defined. The present study has not attempted the impossible task of trying to reconcile all the differing opinions on these matters and it has tried to avoid imposing on Rimbaud yet another preconceived view. It has endeavoured instead to perceive some coherent pattern of development in his ideas, his feelings and consequently his work, in the belief that this very coherence lends authority to the pattern thus perceived.

It should be noted that, because this pattern has been traced in some detail and because of limitations of space, it has proved necessary to omit the chapter on Rimbaud's literary reputation and the selection of critical views which, in accordance with the usual practice in this series, would otherwise have been included.

The University, Aberdeen   C.C.

CONTENTS

to N O' B

THE BIOGRAPHICAL BACKGROUND

If heredity and environment are the two factors which govern psychological development, Arthur Rimbaud's lonely and troubled life can be seen as an inevitable consequence of the circumstances of his birth and childhood. His father was an army officer who, while garrisoned at Charleville on the north-eastern frontier of France in 1853, perhaps feeling that at the age of thirty-eight it was time he settled down, met and married Vitalie Cuif, ten years his junior and the only daughter of a fairly prosperous farmer. But despite this financially comfortable background, Vitalie had had her fair share of hardship in that her mother had died at an early age and she had been forced to take on the task of looking after not only her father but also two brothers, both of whom, perhaps because of these circumstances, were of a decidedly unstable character. Marriage with Captain Rimbaud must have seemed to her, at the age of twenty-eight, like the end of a long, hard road, so her disappointment must have been all the greater when it quickly became apparent that her husband was going to spend far more time away from Charleville, garrisoned in other towns or fighting in the Crimean War, than at home with his wife and the four children, Frédéric, Arthur, Vitalie and Isabelle, who were born in rapid succession between 1853 and 1860. Moreover, after that date the break between husband and wife became complete and Captain Rimbaud deserted his family for good, choosing to retire to his native Burgundy when his army career ended, rather than to return to Charleville to try and pick up the threads of a marriage that had clearly proved disastrous.

After seven short years of what could, at best, have been only intermittent happiness, Vitalie Rimbaud, as she now was, thus found herself in an even less enviable position than she had been as Vitalie Cuif. It is therefore scarcely surprising that she should have become a harsh and domineering figure determined to see that her children did not stray from the straight and narrow path to which her two brothers and her husband had failed to keep.

For almost sixteen years she seemed to have succeeded admirably in her efforts to achieve this goal, particularly as far as her second son, Arthur, was concerned. At school he was a model pupil who carried off prizes in every subject with consummate ease and who seemed clearly destined for a distinguished career. Beneath the surface, however, a spirit of rebellion was beginning to simmer in Rimbaud with the onset of adolescence, and perhaps even earlier if the poem 'Les Poètes de sept ans' is to be taken at its face value. But it was not until 29 August 1870, almost exactly two months before his sixteenth birthday, that Rimbaud, 'lui si sage et si tranquille ordinairement' as his mother plaintively wrote in a letter to his teacher Georges Izambard,[1] suddenly ran away to Paris.

In addition to his growing reluctance to tolerate the rigorous discipline his mother imposed on him, two other factors explain Rimbaud's action. The first is that he had begun to write poetry and had indeed had two poems, 'Les Etrennes des orphelins' and 'Première Soirée', published in literary magazines. He had, moreover, sent three further poems, 'Sensation', 'Soleil et chair' and 'Ophélie' to Théodore de Banville three months earlier on 24 May, expressing the hope, in his accompanying letter, that they might be published in the series entitled *Le Parnasse contemporain*. Clearly therefore he wanted to make a career as a poet and if he was to do so it was essential for him to break into the literary circles in Paris. The second and more immediate reason for Rimbaud's sudden departure from Charleville was that the Franco-Prussian war had begun a month earlier in July 1870, and the French army was soon on the retreat as the prelude to the surrender of the Emperor Napoleon III on 2 September at Sedan, a few miles east of Charleville. Communications with Paris were already difficult by 25 August, as Rimbaud complained in a letter to Izambard, and it was no doubt the fear of being completely cut off from the capital which made him decide, four days later, to try and escape from what he regarded as a provincial backwater.

Unfortunately the direct railway line south to Paris had been put out of action by the invading German army and he had first to travel north to Charleroi in Belgium. From there he had only enough money to buy a ticket to St Quentin, fifty miles to the south-west, but he nevertheless stayed on the train for a further seventy miles all the way to Paris where, as he wrote to Izambard on 5 September, he was 'arrêté en descendant de wagon pour n'avoir pas un sou et devoir treize francs de chemin de fer'. Izambard arranged for his release from prison and took him back to stay at his home in Douai for three weeks until a peremptory letter from Madame Rimbaud dated 24 September demanded her son's immediate return to Charleville.

But after little more than a week at home Rimbaud ran away for the second time, again to Charleroi, perhaps with the intention of making another attempt to get to Paris. If this was the case he was even less successful than on the first occasion and his escapade came to an end when he once more sought refuge at Douai with Izambard who again sent him back to his mother at the end of the month. In a letter written to Izambard on 2 November 1870 Rimbaud confirms that he has kept his promise and returned home and adds: 'Je resterai, je resterai. Je n'ai pas promis cela. Mais je le ferai pour mériter votre affection'. Presumably for this reason Rimbaud made no further attempt to run away for the next four months, but on 25 February 1871 he set off for Paris for the third time. On this occasion he succeeded in reaching his goal and stayed there for a fortnight, enjoying the sense of being at the centre of literary life, as is obvious from a letter to his friend Paul Demeny on 17 April giving a list of all the new books he has seen.

It may be that Rimbaud made a fourth attempt to escape from Charleville shortly after this date. A letter written on 15 May 1871 ends with the words 'dans huit jours je serai à Paris peut-être' and his friend Ernest Delahaye alleged that he spent the last half of May in Paris at the time when, in the aftermath of the Franco-Prussian war, the rebellious forces of the Commune were being crushed by Government troops. Rimbaud was undoubtedly left-wing in his political sympathies, as is apparent from several of his early poems and from his active participation in local political affairs during his stay at Douai in September 1870,[2] but there is no specific reference anywhere in Rimbaud's work to this fourth escapade and unless and until such evidence comes to light this particular episode in his life must remain a matter for conjecture.

His next and, in a sense, final break with Charleville came a few months later in September 1871 when, in response to a letter he had written to Paul Verlaine, who had already published two volumes of poetry, the latter invited him to come to Paris. Although he was to return to Charleville on several occasions afterwards, this date marks the beginning, just before his seventeenth birthday, of his independent adult life. Until then it had been a case of running away from home for brief periods; from

now on it was to be a case of living his own life away from Charleville and returning home only occasionally for short intervals.

This meeting with Verlaine also marked a watershed in Rimbaud's life in another more important way. Owing, presumably,
to his disturbed childhood, the absence of his father from the
family circle and his mother's apparent failure to display any
affection for him, Rimbaud seems to have had a homosexual
streak in his nature which may already have been awakened by
an assault he is reputed to have suffered at the hands of a group of
soldiers during one of his visits to Paris.[3] Verlaine too had a homosexual side to his character, although in his case the explanation
probably lies in the excessively feminine atmosphere in which he
was brought up as the long-awaited only child of a doting mother.
Because of these different backgrounds Rimbaud and Verlaine
were complementary to each other, the former starved of affection
and the latter looking for a strong personality on which to lean.
The letters exchanged between them in the spring of 1872, when
Rimbaud returned to Charleville for a brief period, leave no room
for doubt that extremely strong emotional ties existed between
them: 'Aime-moi, protège et donne confiance. Etant très faible
j'ai très besoin de bontés', wrote Verlaine in a letter dated 2 April
1872 and another letter written about a month later ended with
the words: 'Maintenant, salut, revoir, joie, attente de lettres,
attente de Toi. Moi avoir deux fois cette nuit rêvé: Toi, martyr-
iseur d'enfant . . .'.

In the light of such letters it is scarcely surprising that Verlaine's
marriage to the sixteen year old Mathilde Mauté in August 1870
should soon have foundered and the two poets, after having virtually lived together in Paris during the early part of 1872,[4] left
for Belgium on 7 July. From there they crossed the Channel on
7 September and settled in London. But within a few months their
widely different characters, instead of complementing each other,
became a source of conflict. 'L'époux infernal' grew tired of 'la
vierge folle', to use Rimbaud's terms. Although Verlaine was the
older of the two by ten years, so that Rimbaud had much to learn
from him at first, he was also the weaker, so that Rimbaud must
soon have realized that Verlaine had no positive contribution to
make to their relationship: 'Hélas, je dépendais bien de lui,' says
Verlaine to Rimbaud in the latter's *Une Saison en enfer*, 'mais que
voulait-il avec mon existence terne et lâche. . . Tristement dépitée
je lui dis quelquefois: "Je te comprends". Il haussait les épaules. . .

Je lui faisais promettre qu'il ne me lâcherait pas. Il l'a faite vingt fois, cette promesse d'amant. C'était aussi frivole que moi lui disant: "Je te comprends" '.

It was no doubt this increasing lack of mutual understanding that led them to leave London early in April 1873 and to go their separate ways, Verlaine to his relatives at Jehonville in south-eastern Belgium and Rimbaud to Charleville or, strictly speaking, to the family farm at Roche, a few miles away, where he began *Une Saison en enfer* which is dated 'avril-août 1873'. Although the fact that he had begun this work, which is essentially one of disillusionment, would seem to suggest that the relationship between him and Verlaine was at an end, the two poets nevertheless made one last attempt to come together again, on Verlaine's initiative. 'Pour l'instant je t'embrasse bien,' wrote Verlaine on 18 May 1873, 'et compte sur une bien prochaine entrevue dont tu me donnes l'espoir pour cette semaine. Dès que tu me feras signe, j'y serai.' Six days later, on 24 May 1873 they met at Bouillon, just inside the Belgian frontier halfway between Roche and Jehonville, and from there they left once again for London.

A little over a month later, on 3 July 1873, a particularly violent quarrel flared up between them and Verlaine rushed off to Brussels, threatening to commit suicide if he could not effect a reconciliation with his wife. On the cross-Channel steamer he wrote to Rimbaud: 'Tu dois, au fond comprendre, enfin, qu'il me fallait absolument partir, que cette vie violente et toute de scènes sans motif que ta fantaisie ne pouvait m'aller foutre plus. . . Si d'ici à trois jours, je ne suis pas r'avec ma femme, dans des conditions parfaites, je me brûle la gueule.' But when his wife failed to respond to his appeal to her, Verlaine's intention of shooting himself quickly faded, to be replaced by the rather less alarming decision to go off and join in the fighting that had broken out in the newly proclaimed Spanish Republic. This information too was communicated to Rimbaud in a telegram dated 8 July reading: 'Volontaire Espagne. Viens ici, hôtel Liégois. Blanchisseuse, manuscrits, si possible.' But this dream of death or glory also faded very rapidly and when Rimbaud duly arrived, no doubt with Verlaine's laundry and manuscripts as requested, the latter demanded that they should pick up the threads of their relationship once more. Rimbaud adamantly refused to do this, despite Verlaine's pleas, and on 10 July the latter's wildly erratic behaviour and obvious mental instability came to a climax. He bought a revolver and fired two shots at Rimbaud in their hotel room, hitting him in the wrist. Typically, he was immediately filled with remorse for what he had done and took Rimbaud to hospital to have his wound attended to. Later that same day however, on the way to the railway station, since Rimbaud persisted in his intention of returning to Charleville, Verlaine pulled out his revolver again, or at least appeared to do so to Rimbaud, who called a nearby policeman for help and Verlaine was arrested.

Although Rimbaud, in a statement made to the police on 19 July tried to have the charges dropped, Verlaine nevertheless had to stand trial and on 8 August was condemned to two years imprisonment, a relatively heavy penalty that was due to the prejudice felt against him because of his relationship with Rimbaud. Meanwhile the latter had returned to Roche late in July to finish writing *Une Saison en enfer*, presumably in a state of even deeper disillusionment and distress than when he had begun it some three months before. This traumatic experience may well have put an end to Rimbaud's life as a poet (the complicated question of the date of the *Illuminations* will be discussed in a later chapter) but it did not put an end to his vagabond existence. In the spring of 1874 he set off for London once more, this time in the company of another young poet, Germain Nouveau, although the two parted company soon afterwards. In July Mme Rimbaud came to London accompanied by her younger daughter Vitalie, whose diary records various details of their stay, including Rimbaud's attempts to find a job.[5] He finally obtained a teaching post in Reading but soon tired of it and early in November inserted an advertisement in *The Times* looking for an opportunity to travel 'in southern and eastern countries'. The advertisement did not have the desired effect, but Rimbaud nevertheless gave up his teaching post and for the next few years 'l'homme aux semelles de vent', as Verlaine called him, drifted aimlessly and restlessly through Europe and out to the Far East.[6]

These wanderings began with a few weeks spent in Stuttgart in the spring of 1875, ostensibly to learn German, after which Rimbaud travelled through Switzerland to Milan before returning to Charleville via Marseilles and Paris. In the spring of the following year he went to Austria and from there to Belgium and Holland where he joined the Dutch colonial army. He sailed for Java in July but deserted as soon as he got there and worked his passage back to Europe on a ship with the singularly appropriate name of

The Wandering Chief. In the spring of the year 1877 he turned up at Bremen in Germany where he went to the American consulate and applied, unsuccessfully, to join the American navy, quoting as one of his qualifications the fact that he had deserted, not from the Dutch army, but from the French army, and, even more oddly, naming as his regiment the 47th, which was in fact the one to which his father had belonged.[7] In the summer of that year he is reputed to have been in Scandinavia and presumably returned to Charleville for the winter, according to the pattern which his life tended to follow at this period.

He may well have stayed there throughout the summer since the next definite date furnished by his correspondence is a reference to his departure from Charleville on 20 October 1878. This marks the beginning of a new phase in his life since he now headed for the Middle East and East Africa and his annual hibernation in Charleville came to an end. The various stages in these new wanderings are marked by his arrival in Genoa on 17 November 1878, in Alexandria ten days later and in Cyprus on 16 December where he stayed for six months working as a foreman in a quarry. Towards the end of June 1879 he moved south down the Red Sea and for the next twelve years he worked as a trader in Aden and in the town of Harar in the centre of Abyssinia, as Ethiopia was then called. Early in 1891 he fell ill and on 7 April he had to leave Harar, where he had settled for the previous three years, and have himself carried down to the coast on a stretcher.[8] From there he crossed the Red Sea to Aden but the medical facilities in what was no more than a port of call for ships passing to and from the Suez canal were inadequate to deal with his case, so he sailed for Marseilles where he was taken straight into hospital and his right leg was amputated on 27 May. The amputation had however come too late to check the growth of the cancer from which he was suffering and although he left hospital on 23 July and returned to his family at Roche he was clearly a dying man. On 23 August he made his last journey when he persisted in leaving Roche in the belief that if only he could return to the warmth of East Africa this would somehow cure him. But by the time he reached Marseilles, accompanied by his sister Isabelle, he was so ill that he had to be taken to the hospital from which he had been discharged a month earlier. There his life slowly and painfully ebbed away for over two long months of which his sister has left a moving account in several letters she wrote to her mother.[9] Isabelle's letter of 28 October

1891 is of particular interest because it is in this letter that she tells how Rimbaud agreed that one of the hospital chaplains should hear his confession and of the chaplain's reaction afterwards: 'Quand le prêtre est sorti, il m'a dit, en me regardant d'un air troublé, d'un air étrange: "Votre frère a la foi, mon enfant; que nous disiez-vous donc? Il a la foi, et je n'ai même jamais vu de foi de cette qualité".' It is difficult to believe that Isabelle could have invented this episode, either as a piece of wishful thinking, or as an attempt to console her mother. But on the other hand it is equally difficult to decide how much importance should be attached to this apparent return to Christianity of a dying man. Some may consider such a surrender to be out of keeping with Rimbaud's rebellious spirit; others may consider it as his ultimate recognition of the refuge from reality that he had been seeking all his life; others again may consider it as no more than the delirium of a man who was on the point of death and whose life finally came to an end two weeks later on 10 November 1891.

II

THE EARLY POETRY: 1870–1871

Difficulties of publication

Rimbaud's career as a poet may be said to have begun, if one excludes his school exercises in French and Latin, on 2 January 1870, some two months after his fifteenth birthday, with the publication in a magazine called *La Revue pour Tous* of 'Les Etrennes des orphelins'. Within the next two years he wrote over forty poems of which only one was published, 'Première Soirée', in another magazine called *La Charge* on 13 August 1870. His attempt to persuade Théodore de Banville, in his letter of 23 May 1870, to publish the three poems 'Sensation', 'Ophélie' and 'Credo in unam' (later to be entitled 'Soleil et chair') ended in failure, as did any other efforts he may have made to get his work published. For many years, therefore, until long after he had given up writing, these early poems remained in manuscript form in the hands of various people to whom he had either sent them or given them. The largest collection of these manuscripts was owned by a friend named Paul Demeny for whom Rimbaud copied out twenty-two poems in October 1870 while he was at Douai after his Parisian escapades and to whom he sent a further six poems in letters written in May and June 1871. He also gave additional copies of eight of these poems to his teacher, Georges Izambard, and further copies of the three he sent to Banville remained in the latter's hands along with another poem, 'Ce qu'on dit au poète à propos de fleurs', that Rimbaud sent to him in a letter dated 15 August 1871. Paul Verlaine copied out eleven poems, only two of which figure in the other groups, and the remaining poems found their way into various hands. It was not until 1883 that Verlaine took the lead in publishing some of this early work in a short article on Rimbaud in the magazine *Lutèce* as one of three essays on contemporary writers (the others being Tristan Corbière and Stéphane Mallarmé) under the collective title *Les Poètes maudits*, which were published in volume form the following year. Further poems then came to light and were published in various magazines over the course of the next half-dozen years until finally, and ironically, at the end of 1891, a few weeks after

Rimbaud's death, the first, very incomplete edition of his collected poems was published under the title *Le Reliquaire*. Since then, various editions have brought other poems to light and it now seems fairly certain that all the poetry that Rimbaud wrote in 1870 and 1871 has at last been published.

Revolt and escape

The earliest of these poems, not surprisingly in view of Rimbaud's age, clearly reveal the influence of the older generation of poets writing at the time. The opening words of 'Les Etrennes des orphelins': 'La chambre est pleine d'ombre . . .' obviously echo the opening words of Victor Hugo's 'Les Pauvres Gens': 'Le logis est plein d'ombre . . .' – a shrewd piece of borrowing on Rimbaud's part since 'Les Pauvres Gens' had just been published in the magazine to which he sent 'Les Etrennes des orphelins'. François Coppée's 'Enfants trouvés' has also been suggested as a probable source for Rimbaud's first published poem, along with 'L'Ange et l'enfant' by a much less well-known poet, Jean Reboul. Two other poets, Alfred de Musset and Théodore de Banville, also seem to be echoed here and there in Rimbaud's first attempts at writing poetry, particularly in two of the poems sent to Banville in May 1870, 'Soleil et chair' and 'Ophélie'.

But despite the inevitable influence of established writers in these and other poems it also seems possible to detect in them the first stirrings of Rimbaud's own ideas and emotions which quickly grew in strength and intensity during the months of 1870 and 1871 and soon became channelled into two different but related currents, one leading towards revolt against the restraints of the world around him and the other leading towards escape from those restraints into a world of total freedom.

Bearing in mind that adolescence had just begun for Rimbaud and that it must inevitably have clashed with the austere discipline imposed by Madame Rimbaud, it is not to be wondered at that one of the restraints against which he quickly rebelled was the attitude of the Christian religion towards sex. This is already apparent in 'Soleil et chair', for however great the influence of other writers may be in this poem, it seems certain that Rimbaud shared their attitude and that the view forcefully and succinctly expressed in the following lines is very much his own:

Je crois en toi! je crois en toi! Divine mère,
Aphrodité marine!—Oh! la route est amère
Depuis que l'autre Dieu nous attelle à sa croix . . .

The original title of the poem, 'Credo in unam', significantly and
audaciously alters the opening words of the Nicene Creed by substituting belief in one goddess for belief in one God and in the
course of the poem the redemption of man is seen as being brought
about not through Christ but through Venus:

Tu viendras lui donner la Rédemption sainte!
Splendide, radieuse, au sein des grandes mers
Tu surgiras, jetant sur le vaste Univers
L'Amour infini dans un infini sourire!

A similar attitude to Christianity on this issue, though couched
in very different terms, emerges from the satirical short story, *Un
Cœur sous une soutane*, which Rimbaud wrote at about the same time
as 'Soleil et chair'. These 'intimités d'un séminariste', as the story
is sub-titled, poke fun at the way a young priest sublimates his
sexuality and turns to Christianity for consolation after being
rejected by the girl he loves: 'N'ayant plus celle que j'aime, je vais
aimer la foi'.

A year later Rimbaud returned to this question in a very different mood in 'Les Premières Communions', dated July 1871, where
the theme of a natural and healthy sensuality being warped and
corrupted is powerfully argued by a girl who is about to take her
first communion, as Rimbaud's sister Isabelle had done the previous May and as he himself had done a few years before, and who
reverses the argument of the seminarist in *Un Cœur sous une soutane*,
protesting that the Christian faith has taken hold of her and that
she is now no longer capable of human love:

J'étais bien jeune et Christ a souillé mes haleines.
Il me bonda jusqu'à la gorge de dégoûts! . . .
Et mon cœur et ma chair par ta chair embrassée
Fourmillent du baiser putride de Jésus!

But Rimbaud rebelled against Christianity not only because of
the tyranny it exercised over the individual; he objected with a
similarly increasing violence to the tyranny it exercised over
society. In the sonnet 'Le Mal', which was among those copied
out at Douai in October 1870, the Church is depicted as a wealthy
institution interested only in the money that the faithful con-
tribute:

Il est un Dieu qui rit aux nappes damassées
Des autels, à l'encens, aux grands calices d'or;
Qui dans le bercement des hosannah s'endort,

Et se réveille, quand des mères, ramassées
Dans l'angoisse, et pleurant sous leur vieux bonnet noir,
Lui donnent un gros sou lié dans leur mouchoir!

Some six months later his growing impatience with the submissive attitude of the poor towards the Church is apparent in 'Les Pauvres à l'église':

Heureux, humiliés comme des chiens battus,
Les Pauvres au bon Dieu, le patron et le sire,
Tendent leurs oremus risibles et têtus,

and towards the end of the poem he paints a bitter portrait of the wealthy women of Charleville welcomed by the Church:

. . . des nefs où périt le soleil, plis de soie
Banals, sourires verts, les Dames des quartiers
Distingués—ô Jesus!—les malades du foie
Font baiser leurs longs doigts jaunes aux bénitiers.

These poems attacking the Church as a *bourgeois* institution are clearly linked with another poem, 'A la musique', written in the summer of 1870, where Rimbaud sardonically sketches the pompous citizens of Charleville listening to a military band in the station square:

Sur la place taillée en mesquines pelouses,
Square où tout est correct, les arbres et les fleurs,
Tous les bourgeois poussifs qu'étranglent les chaleurs
Portent, les jeudis soirs, leurs bêtises jalouses.

—L'orchestre militaire, au milieu du jardin,
Balance ses schakos dans la *Valse des Fifres*:
—Autour, aux premiers rangs, parade le gandin;
Le notaire pend à ses breloques à chiffres.

In view of this antipathy towards the *bourgeoisie* it was inevitable that the spirit of revolt in the adolescent Rimbaud should take on a political aspect in the circumstances which prevailed in France in 1870, with the power of Napoleon III being rapidly eroded and finally swept away at Sedan. This can be perceived, if only indirectly, in the admiring portrait he draws, in 'Le Forgeron', of the leader of the revolutionary mob in 1792:

Le bras sur un marteau gigantesque, effrayant
D'ivresse et de grandeur, le front vaste, riant
Comme un clairon d'airain avec toute sa bouche,
Et prenant ce gros-là dans son regard farouche,
Le Forgeron parlait à Louis Seize . . .

His Republican sympathies were openly revealed in a number of poems copied out, like 'Le Forgeron', in October 1870. One of these, 'Morts de quatre-vingt-douze . . .', specifically links the events of 1792 and of 1870 in a ferocious attack on those who had the effrontery, as Rimbaud saw it, to appeal to Republicans to bury their differences with the Bonapartists and rally to the defence of the Second Empire, as their forefathers had rallied to the defence of France almost a century before. 'Ma patrie se lève', he wrote to Izambard on 25 August 1870, 'moi, j'aime mieux la voir assise', and he poked fun at all those who 'chassepot au cœur, font du patrouillotisme'. This is also the theme of a second political sonnet 'L'éclatante victoire de Sarrebruck' in which he ridiculed the patriotic pride his countrymen displayed as a result of a French victory in a minor frontier skirmish on 2 August 1870. The essential thing for Rimbaud was that Napoleon III should be toppled from his throne, and in a third political sonnet, 'Rages de Césars', written after the overwhelming defeat at Sedan, he clearly derived considerable satisfaction from portraying the Emperor's impotent rage as he paced up and down the grounds of the castle in which he was held prisoner:

L'Homme pâle, le long des pelouses fleuries,
Chemine, en habit noir, et le cigare aux dents:
L'Homme pâle repense aux fleurs des Tuileries
—Et parfois son œil terne a des regards ardents . . .

Car l'Empereur est soûl de ses vingt ans d'orgie!
Il s'était dit: 'Je vais souffler la Liberté
Bien délicatement, ainsi qu'une bougie!'
La Liberté revit! Il se sent éreinté . . .

The fall of the Second Empire did not, however, lead, as Rimbaud had hoped, to the establishment of the kind of left-wing republic that he favoured and the defeat of the Commune in May 1871 inspired him to write his fourth and last political poem, 'L'Orgie parisienne ou Paris se repeuple', in which he bitterly reviled those who had fled from the capital while it had been ruled by the revolutionary organization of the Commune and who flooded back into the city after the victory of the government forces.[1]

This rebellious attitude was not something that Rimbaud reserved for matters of major importance such as religion and politics. In the details of everyday life too he was constantly impatient of authority. The sonnet 'Les Douaniers' reveals his contempt for customs officers; the longer poem 'Les Assis' displays what Verlaine was to call his 'puissance d'ironie' and his 'verve terrible' as he pours scorn on librarians, as a consequence of having crossed swords with the one at Charleville; and 'Les Poètes de sept ans' describes, with a wealth of detail, the early simmering of his revolt against the authority of his mother. But however ready Rimbaud may have been to rebel against authority in any shape or form, it would nevertheless be wrong to conclude that his early poetry contains nothing but scorn and derision. He also had a softer side to his nature and the rough treatment he meted out to those who held the upper hand in society was matched by the concern he expressed for the poor and the handicapped. In 'Les Poètes de sept ans' he writes:

> . . . Ces enfants seuls étaient ses familiers
> Qui, chétifs, fronts nus, œil déteignant sur la joue
> Cachant de maigres doigts jaunes et noirs de boue
> Sous des habits puant la foire et tout vieillots,
> Conversaient avec la douceur des idiots!

'Les Effarés' reveals his sympathy for these same children clustering round the basement window of a bakery and an equal sympathy for the mothers of such children can be perceived in 'Les Pauvres à l'église'. In 'Le Mal' his portrayal of God as a callous and cynical figure, uninterested in the sufferings of the poor, is in sharp contrast with the evident sorrow that he feels at the death of so many soldiers in the Franco-Prussian War. This same theme is picked up again in the sonnet 'Le Dormeur du val' where the tranquil picture of a young soldier lying beside a stream is gradually altered as a sense of stillness and coldness steals over the tercets and is finally and brutally destroyed by the last line of the poem:

> Les pieds dans les glaïeuls, il dort. Souriant comme
> Sourirait un enfant malade, il fait un somme:
> Nature, berce-le chaudement: il a froid.

> Les parfums ne font pas frissonner sa narine;
> Il dort dans le soleil, la main sur sa poitrine
> Tranquille. Il a deux trous rouges au côté droit.

This feeling of pity for others could, at times, turn into a feeling of pity for himself. This is already apparent in 'Les Etrennes des orphelins', if it is accepted that the poem is not solely a pastiche of Hugo, Coppée and Reboul but that there is also some element of personal experience in the pathetic account of children deprived of parental care. But it is particularly evident in 'Les Chercheuses de poux', probably written in September 1870 when Rimbaud, after the few days in prison that resulted from his first Parisian escapade, went to stay with Izambard for three weeks at Douai. According to the latter's account, it is his two aunts who figure in the poem as the 'deux grandes sœurs charmantes' who undertake the task of de-lousing Rimbaud and thus awaken in him a desolate sense of self-pity:

> L'enfant se sent, selon la lenteur des caresses,
> Sourdre et mourir sans cesse un désir de pleurer.

This was, however, one of the rare occasions when Rimbaud was able to find in the world of reality the care and protection that, beneath his outer shell of anger and revolt, he no doubt needed as much as any boy of sixteen. For the most part he could seek consolation and comfort only in a dream world, and a significant number of his early poems are concerned with this theme of escape from reality. As early as 'Les Etrennes des orphelins' this can be seen to be the case:

> . . . l'ange des berceaux vient essuyer leurs yeux,
> Et dans ce lourd sommeil met un rêve joyeux,
> Un rêve si joyeux que leur lèvre mi-close,
> Souriante semblait murmurer quelque chose . . .

In 'Sensation' too, written in March 1870, Rimbaud, looking forward to the summer, dreams of wandering freely through the countryside:

> Par les soirs bleus d'été, j'irai dans les sentiers,
> Picoté par les blés, fouler l'herbe menue;
> Rêveur, j'en sentirai la fraîcheur à mes pieds.
> Je laisserai le vent baigner ma tête nue.

> Je ne parlerai pas, je ne penserai rien;
> Mais l'amour infini me montera dans l'âme,
> Et j'irai loin, bien loin, comme un bohémien,
> Par la Nature,—heureux comme avec une femme.

A few months later, in one of the best-known of his early poems,
'Ma Bohème', written in the autumn of 1870, this romantic dream
was in part fulfilled, as far as wandering through the countryside
was concerned, although the companionship of a woman was
something that still remained in the realm of his imagination:

> Je m'en allais, les poings dans mes poches crevées;
> Mon paletot aussi devenait idéal;
> J'allais sous le ciel, Muse! et j'étais ton féal;
> Oh! là! là! que d'amours splendides j'ai rêvées! . . .

In 'Rêvé pour l'hiver' too, as the title suggests, a lonely railway
journey in the autumn of 1870 inspires a romantic dream of a
future railway journey when Rimbaud will no longer be alone:

> L'hiver, nous irons dans un petit wagon rose
>   Avec des coussins bleus.
> Nous serons bien. Un nid de baisers fous repose
>   Dans chaque coin mœlleux . . .

On occasions his dreams could take on a less tender note, as in 'A
la musique', the final line of which – 'Et mes désirs brutaux
s'accrochent à leurs lèvres' – so shocked Izambard that he per-
suaded his pupil to tone it down considerably, with the result that
the insipid modified version – 'Et je sens les baisers qui me vien-
nent aux lèvres' – is quite out of keeping with the cynical sensuality of the earlier stanzas.

Rimbaud's relationship with women in the poems of 1870 thus
remains imaginary rather than real, perhaps because of some
innate psychological difficulty in transforming the dream into
reality. It is no doubt as a consequence of this that by June 1871
he rejects the idea of finding comfort and consolation in the companionship of women, if one is to judge by the attitude of the
young man in 'Les Sœurs de charité' who must surely be Rimbaud himself:

> Le jeune homme, devant les laideurs de ce monde
> Tressaille dans son cœur largement irrité,
> Et plein de la blessure éternelle et profonde
> Se prend à desirer sa sœur de charité.

Mais, ô Femme, monceau d'entrailles, pitié douce,
Tu n'es jamais la sœur de charité, jamais . . .

It was probably at about this date too that Rimbaud wrote *Les
Déserts de l'amour*, a title which clearly implies an attitude similar
to that of 'Les Sœurs de charité' and which arises from the fact
that in this short prose text he describes two dreams in which 'un
tout jeune homme' imagines himself the victim of two unhappy
sexual encounters. These dreams are preceded by an 'Avertissement' in which he declares that 'n'ayant pas aimé de femmes, —
quoique plein de sang!—il eut son âme et son cœur, toute sa
force, élevés en des erreurs étranges et tristes'. Suzanne Bernard
sees in these lines a veiled allusion to Rimbaud's homosexuality,
which may have come to the surface at this time,[2] but Antoine
Adam argues that they simply mean that, because of his failure
with women, Rimbaud's energies were turned away from reality
towards a dream world.[3]

Whether or not one accepts Adam's interpretation it is undoubtedly true that the harsh reality of life became increasingly
intolerable for Rimbaud in 1870 and 1871 and it is not therefore
surprising that he should have escaped into an increasingly
exotic world of his own creation. This is precisely what he does
towards the end of 'Les Poètes de sept ans', dated 25 May 1871,
after rebelling in vain against all the restrictions and constraints
of life in Charleville:

Il rêvait la prairie amoureuse, où les houles
Lumineuses, parfums sains, pubescences d'or,
Font leur remuement calme et prennent leur essor . . .

Clearly it was in his vivid imagination that he could best find an
alternative to the real world and the final lines of 'Les Poètes de
sept ans' conjure up a striking picture of him alone in an attic
room, isolated from the sounds of life in the town below and transforming the pieces of coarse linen on which he is lying into the
sails of ships setting off for distant seas:

Il lisait son roman sans cesse médité,
Plein de lourds ciels ocreux et de forêts noyées,
De fleurs de chair aux bois sidérals déployées,
Vertige, écroulements, déroutes et pitié!
—Tandis que se faisait la rumeur du quartier,
En bas, —seul, et couché sur des pièces de toile
Ecrue, et pressentant violemment la voile!

Although these lines are dated 26 May 1871, they contain within them the germ of the most celebrated of Rimbaud's poems which he was to write a few months later, 'Le Bateau ivre', where his gift for escaping into a dream world by transforming reality out of all recognition is carried to extreme lengths. For there can be little doubt that it is his escapades of the previous autumn and winter that form the basis on which he builds up the fantastic imagery with which the poem is filled:

> Dans les clapotements furieux des marées,
> Moi, l'autre hiver, plus sourd que les cerveaux d'enfants,
> Je courus! Et les Peninsules démarrées
> N'ont pas subi tohus-bohus plus triomphants . . .

The function of the image of the boat plunging rudderless through countless seas, dancing like a cork on the waves, encountering giant serpents and sea-monsters, icebergs and waterspouts, is to convey the intense excitement and almost delirious happiness Rimbaud had experienced during his brief spells of freedom:

> Je sais les cieux crevant en éclairs, et les trombes
> Et les ressacs et les courants: je sais le soir,
> L'Aube exaltée ainsi qu'un peuple de colombes,
> Et j'ai vu quelquefois ce que l'homme a cru voir . . .

Towards the end of 'Le Bateau ivre', however, after seventeen stanzas extolling the idea of total freedom, the paradoxical longing for shelter and protection already revealed in such poems as 'Les Chercheuses de poux' re-appears. The boat may have been glad to leave the old continent of Europe, Rimbaud may have been glad to leave the home in which he lived for sixteen years, anyone may be glad to be no longer stuck in the same old rut, but nevertheless there is inevitably a tinge of regret for the stable and sheltered existence that has been left behind:

> Fileur éternel des immobilités bleues,
> Je regrette l'Europe aux anciens parapets! . . .

But having enjoyed the exhilarating taste of freedom Rimbaud feels that it is there that his future activity must lie:

> J'ai vu des archipels sidéraux! et des îles
> Dont les cieux délirants sont ouverts au vogueur:
> —Est-ce en ces nuits sans fonds que tu dors et t'exiles,
> Million d'oiseaux d'or, ô future Vigueur? . . .

As the poem draws towards its conclusion he acknowledges that he has agonized over his predicament long enough; each new dawn now brings fresh despair; as night succeeds day his bitterness increases; he is filled with renewed longing to set off again and to feel once more the exhilaration of drifting freely along:

> Mais, vrai, j'ai trop pleuré! Les Aubes sont navrantes
> Toute lune est atroce et tout soleil amer:
> L'âcre amour m'a gonflé de torpeurs enivrantes.
> O que ma quille éclate! O que j'aille à la mer! . . .

Only if he were still a child could he accept, with sadness and resignation, the restrictions imposed upon him by life at home; only if the boat were a toy boat could it sail within the confines of a pond:

> Si je désire une eau d'Europe, c'est la flache
> Noire et froide où vers le crepuscule embaumé
> Un enfant accroupi plein de tristesses, lâche
> Un bateau frêle comme un papillon de mai . . .

But he is no longer a child; he has known the joys of freedom and he is now no longer prepared to follow in the wake of others, to pursue a set course marked out for him, to sail under surveillance:[4]

> Je ne puis plus, baigné de vos langueurs, ô lames,
> Enlever leur sillage aux porteurs de cotons,
> Ni traverser l'orgueil des drapeaux et des flammes,
> Ni nager sous les yeux horribles des pontons.

Rimbaud was as good as his word and early in September 1871, in response to an invitation from Verlaine to whom he had written, he was to set off for Paris to begin the second phase of his career as a poet.

The 'lettre du voyant' and after

The spirit of revolt and desire for freedom that can be perceived in these early poems is matched by a certain unconventionality in their language. 'Merde à ces chiens-là' is the unusually realistic expression of defiance used by the revolutionary blacksmith in 'Le Forgeron'; the children in 'Les Effarés' are described as crouching down 'leurs culs en rond'; the choir in 'Les Pauvres à l'église' is defined as 'vingt gueules gueulant des cantiques pieux'; the waitress in 'Au Cabaret vert' is 'la fille aux tétons énormes'; and in

'Oraison du soir' Rimbaud 'pisse vers les cieux bruns, très haut et très loin'.

Yet despite the suggestion of impatience with the formal restraints of conventional verse implicit in these occasional audacities, Rimbaud's early poems, on the whole, remain cast very much in the classical mould. Whether unfolding a story as in 'Le Forgeron', or going into descriptive detail as in 'A la musique', or putting across a political message as in 'Morts de quatre-vingt-douze', or developing philosophical ideas as in 'Soleil et chair' they are firmly and clearly organized. Furthermore the rhymes bear witness to the care with which they have been chosen and the rhythms too are highly conventional in that three-quarters of the early poems are in alexandrines and one-third of them are sonnets.

Towards the end of this period, however, Rimbaud made an abortive attempt to spread his rebellion against authority and his desire for freedom to matters of form in poetry. On 13 May 1871 he wrote to Georges Izambard a letter containing two paragraphs which were to be virtually repeated and greatly expanded in another letter written two days later on 15 May 1871 to Paul Demeny. This was what has come to be known as the 'lettre du voyant' in which Rimbaud contended that the true poet must be a seer capable of looking beyond the real world. 'Je veux être poète et je travaille à me rendre *voyant*', he wrote in the first of the two letters, and in the second: 'Je dis qu'il faut être *voyant*, se faire *voyant*'. In advancing these ideas he was no doubt influenced by the Romantic poets in general and in particular by Victor Hugo, but he must have owed a still greater debt to Baudelaire who had declared that 'c'est à travers la poésie que l'âme entrevoit les splendeurs situées derrière le tombeau'. But Rimbaud then parted company from his predecessors by arguing that the poet could achieve his aim of becoming a 'voyant', not through any orderly intellectual process, but by 'le dérèglement de tous les sens', as he put it in the first letter, expanding this slightly in the second letter to form the often-quoted sentence: 'Le poète se fait *voyant* par un long, immense et raisonné *dérèglement* de *tous les sens*'. Further-more, the poet's function is simply to note down the disordered sensations he thus deliberately cultivates without intervening to exercise any conscious control. He is not personally involved in the process since it is a mere accident that he happens to possess this faculty for receiving and transmitting visions of another world. '*JE* est un autre', he wrote in both letters, adding, in the first letter, an analogy with a piece of wood which happens to be a violin: 'Tant pis pour le bois qui se trouve violon', and, in the second letter, a similar analogy with a piece of brass which happens to be a bugle: 'Si le cuivre s'éveille clairon il n'y a rien de sa faute'. He then goes on, in the second letter, to develop further this idea that the poet is a passive instrument which is played upon by forces outside his control: 'J'assiste[5] à l'éclosion de ma pensée: je la regarde, je l'écoute'. All the poet can do is to provide an initial impulse, but thereafter the poem follows its own course at its own pace: 'Je lance un coup d'archet: la symphonie fait son remuement dans les profondeurs ou vient d'un bond sur la scène'.

Rimbaud was therefore determined to abandon in poetry the world of ordered reality and its consciously controlled presentation so as to give free play instead to the disordered world of the imagination. 'Les inventions d'inconnu', he wrote, 'réclament des formes nouvelles'. With splendid arrogance he dismissed all earlier poets, from the ancient Greeks to the French Romantics, as mere 'versificateurs', among whom Racine, with his beautifully balanced alexandrines, was the 'Divin Sot'. 'Tout est prose rimée, un jeu', he insisted, and even among the Romantics, some of whom seemed to him to possess that vision of another world that is the hallmark of the true poet, he condemned Lamartine as being 'étranglé par la forme vieille', poured scorn on Musset's poetry as 'de la peinture à l'émail, de la poésie solide', and reprimanded Baudelaire, whom he otherwise admired as 'le premier voyant, roi des poètes, un vrai Dieu', for the unadventurous form of his poetry.

Yet Rimbaud's own first attempts enclosed in the two 'lettres du voyant', at giving free rein to his poetic imagination, are largely failures because, paradoxically, though not perhaps surprisingly in one so young, he stuck firmly to traditionally rigid patterns of rhyme and rhythm, so that the words he uses and the ideas he expresses, far from flowing freely, are to a considerable extent dictated by these factors. This at least seems to be the explanation of such nonsense verses as the following typical quatrain from the first of the poems included in the 'lettre du voyant' of 15 May, 'Chant de guerre parisien':

> Ils ont schako, sabre et tam-tam,
> Non la vieille boîte à bougies,
> Et des yoles qui n'ont jam, jam . . .
> Fendent le lac aux eaux rougies.

It seems certain that the third line is an inconsequential echo of the well-known song: 'Il était un petit navire, / Qui n'avait jam, jam, jamais navigué' and that its sole function is to make up an eight syllable line and to provide a rhyme for 'tam-tam' which is itself, in a poem whose 'coup d'archet' is the siege of Paris during the Commune, an inappropriate modification of the normal word 'tambour'. Similarly the adjective 'rougies' appears to have slipped in simply as a rhyme for 'bougies' and it is now generally agreed that the whole of the fourth line is meaningless within the context of the poem and that it cannot refer, as was at one time suggested, to the lake in the Bois de Boulogne since this was not captured by government troops until the very day that the 'lettre du voyant' was written when Rimbaud, in Charleville, could not yet have received the news from Paris.[6]

In the second poem enclosed in the letter of 15 May, 'Mes petites amoureuses', which Rimbaud prefaces with the remark: 'J'ai l'archet en main, je commence . . .', echoing his earlier phrase: 'Je lance un coup d'archet . . .', it seems equally apparent that, once he had launched the initial theme indicated in the title, certain words called to his mind certain other words rhyming with them which he proceeded to use without reference to their meaning:

Nous nous aimions à cette époque   Un soir tu me sacras poète,
  Bleu laideron!   Blond laideron:
On mangeait des œufs à la coque Descends ici que je te fouette
  Et du mouron!   En mon giron.

  J'ai dégueulé ta bandoline,
    Noir laideron;
  Tu couperais ma mandoline
    Au fil du front . . .

The line 'on mangeait des œufs à la coque' no doubt sprang to his mind because it had eight syllables and because it provided a rhyme for 'époque', although it also makes at least some sort of sense, which is more than can be said of the following line, 'et du mouron', since chickweed is not normally eaten with hard-boiled eggs. But it does provide a rhyme for 'laideron', as does 'giron', which otherwise seems inexplicable, and as does 'au fil du front', which seems to have been called to mind by the use of the word 'couper' and by some kind of association with the expression 'au fil de l'épée'. Similarly 'mandoline' is an obvious rhyme for 'bandoline' since only one letter is changed, but it makes little or no sense to associate a musical instrument with hair cream.

The third poem which Rimbaud wrote along these lines, 'Le Cœur supplicié', later entitled 'Le Cœur du pitre' and later still 'Le Cœur volé', was not enclosed with the other two in the letter of 15 May to Paul Demeny but in the shorter letter of 13 May to Georges Izambard. Rimbaud prefaces it with the remark: 'Est-ce de la poésie? C'est de la fantaisie toujours', and he adds at the end of the poem: 'Cela ne veut pas rien dire', suggesting that an initial 'coup d'archet' has been allowed to develop along lines which could lead the inattentive reader into mistakenly thinking that the poem was totally devoid of meaning. What this 'coup d'archet' is seems to be indicated, as with the other two poems, by the title, or rather by the successive titles – Rimbaud has been deeply hurt emotionally, he has felt himself to be an object of ridicule, his capacity for affection has been stolen from him. Whether this was a general feeling of revulsion against society as a whole, or whether Rimbaud had in mind some particular incident depends on whether the references in the poem to the obscene jokes of soldiers are taken in a literal or a metaphorical sense. It has been suggested that, during one of his brief visits to Paris during the Commune, especially if his disputed fourth escape from Charleville took place in late April or early May 1871, he may have been sexually assaulted by a troop of soldiers, in which case the opening lines of the poem in particular present few difficulties of interpretation:

> Mon triste cœur bave à la poupe,
> Mon cœur est plein de caporal:
> Ils y lancent des jets de soupe,
> Mon triste cœur bave à la poupe:
> Sous les quolibets de la troupe
> Qui lance un rire général,
> Mon triste cœur bave à la poupe,
> Mon cœur est plein de caporal:

If, however, the 'coup d'archet' is a feeling of disgust with life in general, then words such as 'poupe', 'soupe' and 'troupe' can be explained, as in the case of 'Chant de guerre parisien' and 'Mes petites amoureuses', by Rimbaud's readiness to accept the first rhymes that spring to his mind irrespective of their sense. The second stanza certainly gives the impression of being largely controlled by the rhymes and by the necessity to fill out the lines to make up the requisite eight syllables, although the theme of the first stanza is continued by the reference to an erect phallus and by the use of the familiar word for soldiers – 'pioupious' – especially since the adjectival form created by Rimbaud is modelled on 'soldatesque' which has a pejorative sense suggestive of brutality:

> Ithyphalliques et pioupiesques
> Leurs insultes l'ont dépravé!
> A la vesprée ils font des fresques
> Ithyphalliques et pioupiesques.
> O flots abracadabrantesques,
> Prenez mon cœur, qu'il soit sauvé:
> Ithyphalliques et pioupiesques
> Leurs insultes l'ont dépravé!

Behind the apparent disorder of the images a certain logical development can be perceived as the profound disgust of the first stanza gives way in this second stanza to an intense desire to be cleansed of a sense of outrage. The third stanza too is a mixture of underlying sense and apparent nonsense as Rimbaud wonders what his ultimate reaction will be and yet expresses his doubts in lines which, like those of the second stanza, are clearly dominated by the rhymes and which suggest perhaps a flagging of inspiration, especially in the third, fourth and fifth lines, coupled with an apparent lack of any attempt to work on these lines to try and improve them:

> Quand ils auront tari leurs chiques,
> Comment agir, ô cœur volé?
> Ce seront des refrains bachiques
> Quand ils auront tari leurs chiques:
> J'aurai des sursauts stomachiques
> Si mon cœur triste est ravalé:
> Quand ils auront tari leurs chiques,
> Comment agir, ô cœur volé?

In all three of these poems it seems therefore that although Rimbaud, in accordance with the ideas expressed in the 'lettre du voyant', is trying to extend his desire for complete freedom into the sphere of poetry, he has not yet realized that there is no point in throwing off the shackles of logical thought if one still operates within the confines of rhyme and rhythm. Perhaps for this reason the 'lettre du voyant' does not mark the beginning of a complete change of poetic technique on Rimbaud's part. He may well have felt that the results obtained were not what he had hoped for and during the next few months he was to pursue the old and the new methods in parallel. Even the 'lettre du voyant' itself includes a poem, 'Accroupissements', which is clearly very different from its companion poems. The opening stanza has all those features characteristic of a carefully composed piece of work that are lacking in 'Chant de guerre parisien', 'Mes petites amoureuses' and 'Le cœur supplicié'. It begins with a subordinate clause of time, then the subject is followed by a descriptive phrase which in its turn is qualified and re-qualified so that not until the last line does the main verb of this complex and tightly organized sentence make its appearance. The rhymes, moreover, seem carefully chosen and have none of the air of having been nonchalantly slipped in regardless of their relationship to the sense of the poem:

> Bien tard, quand il se sent l'estomac écœuré,
> Le frère Milotus, un œil à la lucarne
> D'où le soleil, clair comme un chaudron récuré,
> Lui darde une migraine et fait son regard darne,
> Déplace dans les draps son ventre de curé . . .

There is clearly no question here of the poet striking the first note and then allowing the poem to take its course, and it may well be that when Rimbaud prefaced 'Accroupissements' with the phrase: 'Et finissons par un chant pieux', this was not merely a sardonic comment on the subject matter of the poem, but was a no less sardonic comment on the orthodox and 'pious' form of the poem as compared with the unconventionality of the other poems in the 'lettre du voyant'.

About half of the dozen or so poems that Rimbaud wrote after the date of the 'lettre du voyant' and before the end of 1871 are equally conventional in their form and style. 'Les poètes de sept ans', for example, is dated 26 May 1871, but all the brave new ideas of less than a fortnight before seem to have been entirely forgotten in this fairly lengthy narrative poem couched in carefully composed alexandrines. There is no evidence of the poet passively letting his thoughts unfold or of the 'dérèglement de tous les sens' in such lines as the following:

> Il craignait les blafards dimanches de décembre,
> Où, pommadé, sur un guéridon d'acajou,
> Il lisait une Bible à la tranche vert-chou;
> Des rêves l'oppressaient chaque nuit dans l'alcôve.
> Il n'aimait pas Dieu; mais les hommes qu'au soir fauve,

Noirs, en blouse, il voyait rentrer dans le faubourg
Où les crieurs, en trois roulements de tambour,
Font autour des édits rire et gronder la foule . . .

Similarly, the first two verses of 'Les Pauvres à l'église', written later in 1871 at an unspecified date, have so complex a syntax, with a series of adjectival phrases preceding the noun they qualify, that Rimbaud must clearly have devoted a great deal of conscious effort to the composition of these lines:

Parqués entre des bancs de chêne, aux coins d'église
Qu'attiédit puamment leur souffle, tous leurs yeux
Vers le chœur ruisselant d'orrie et la maîtrise
Aux vingt gueules gueulant les cantiques pieux;

Comme un parfum de pain humant l'odeur de cire,
Heureux, humiliés comme des chiens battus,
Les Pauvres au bon Dieu, le patron et le sire,
Tendent leurs oremus risibles et têtus . . .

The syntax of the opening lines of 'Les Sœurs de charité' dated June 1871 is perhaps even more complex and the inversion of subject and object in the third line accompanied by the elegant substitution of a past subjunctive for the more usual conditional make it clear that in this case too Rimbaud was not content merely to 'lancer un coup d'archet' and then allow the poem to develop in its own way:

Le jeune homme dont l'œil est brillant, la peau brune,
Le beau corps de vingt ans qui devrait aller nu,
Et qu'eût, le front cerclé de cuivre, sous la lune,
Adoré, dans la Perse, un Génie inconnu,

Impétueux avec des douceurs virginales
Et noires, fier de ses premiers entêtements,
Pareil aux jeunes mers, pleurs de nuits estivales
Qui se retournent sur des lits de diamants;

Le jeune homme, devant les laideurs de ce monde
Tressaille dans son cœur largement irrité,
Et plein de la blessure éternelle et profonde,
Se prend à désirer sa sœur de charité.

In the case of 'Les Premières Communions', dated July 1871, not only is there an equally involved sentence structure, but the poem as a whole is reminiscent of 'Les Etrennes des orphelins', 'Soleil et chair' and 'Le Forgeron' in that it is a lengthy composition of over one hundred lines divided into a number of sections. These set the scene first of all and then concentrate on the central figure in the poem, the girl who is about to take her first communion, before moving forward into the future to show the effect of the girl's feelings towards the figure of Christ on her feelings towards the man she is to marry. This kind of approach to poetry obviously demands an orderliness of thought rather than a disorderliness of the senses. As for the celebrated sonnet 'Voyelles', a wide variety of suggestions have been put forward to try and explain why Rimbaud should have associated certain colours with the five vowels: 'A noir, E blanc, I rouge, U vert, O bleu . . .', and why he should have then associated these sounds and colours with certain images. Some have argued that Rimbaud was transposing into poetry the colours and pictures of a spelling book he had used as a child; others have claimed that he dabbled in alchemy and that the colours he uses and the order in which they occur have some alchemical significance; one critic felt that it was the shapes of the letters that was of prime importance and that, if one took the liberty of tipping the letter I on its side, it could readily be metamorphosed into Rimbaud's images of a jet of blood, or the line of a mouth, just as the prongs of the letter E, lying on its back, could conjure up his images of tents and glaciers and flowers; another critic radically modified this explanation and by dint of rounding out the corners of the supine letter E saw it as evocative of the shape of a woman's breasts, with the remaining letters referring to other parts of the female body and the sonnet as a whole evoking a sexual experience;[7] the present author has suggested that the images are inspired by the ideas generally associated with the colours Rimbaud uses – black with death and decay, white with purity, red with violence, green with peacefulness and blue with a sense of eternity and infinity.[8] But one thing that these and other explanations have in common is that they assume that the sonnet is a carefully composed piece of work, quite unrelated to the ideas advanced in the 'lettre du voyant'. Finally 'Le Bateau ivre', probably written in September 1871 just before Rimbaud's departure for Paris to join Verlaine, despite its intoxicating welter of images, is rigorously organized into three distinct parts – the first seventeen verses describing the delirious happiness of the rudderless boat swept along at the mercy of the wind and the waves, the next four verses expressing the boat's astonishment that it should nevertheless feel regret for the stable and orderly life

that has been left behind, and the last four verses summarizing the
pros and cons of the argument and reaching a final conclusion.

In view of the elaborate nature of these poems of the latter part
of 1871 it might be thought that Rimbaud abandoned the ideas
he had put forward in the 'lettre du voyant' as soon as he had for-
mulated them. A closer examination, however, suggests that
certain traces of his ideas can be perceived in the welter of images
in 'Le Bateau ivre' referred to above, for although the poem has an
overall framework that has clearly been carefully thought out,
within its three component parts and particularly within the long
first part there is a marked simplicity of structure and style which
enables Rimbaud to pile images pell-mell one on top of the other:

> Je sais les cieux crevant en éclairs, et les trombes
> Et les ressacs et les courants: je sais le soir,
> L'Aube exaltée ainsi qu'un peuple de colombes,
> Et j'ai vu quelquefois ce que l'homme a cru voir!
>
> J'ai vu le soleil bas, taché d'horreurs mystiques,
> Illuminant de longs figements violets,
> Pareils à des acteurs de drames très antiques
> Les flots roulant au loin leurs frissons de volets!
>
> J'ai rêvé la nuit verte aux neiges éblouies,
> Baiser montant aux yeux des mers avec lenteurs,
> La circulation des sèves inouïes,
> Et l'éveil jaune et bleu des phosphores chanteurs!

Some of these images are so unusual that it is difficult to escape
the conclusion that Rimbaud hastily inserted them to suit the
immediate demands of rhyme and rhythm instead of patiently
modifying them so that they would also suit the demands of sense.
In the comparison between the dawn and a flight of doves for
example, strange enough in itself, the words 'un peuple' have
presumably been substituted for 'un vol' or 'une volée' because
neither of the latter expressions has the necessary three syllables.
In the second stanza quoted above the curious metaphor applied
to the waves, 'leurs frissons de volets', may well be explained by
the fact that a ready rhyme with 'violets' is thus provided. In the
third stanza the word 'éblouies' should more properly be 'éblouis-
santes', and the word 'lenteurs' has been oddly pluralized, no
doubt to match the word 'chanteurs' which, in its turn, is an
obvious rhyme for 'lenteurs' even though its association with
'phosphores' is difficult to justify on grounds of meaning.

'Voyelles' too, within the overall framework of the sonnet, adopts this technique of a succession of images with no linking thread running between them and it contains a number of adjectives which provide fairly obvious rhymes but which are far from meaningful in association with the nouns they qualify – 'mouches éclatantes', 'puanteurs cruelles' and 'ivresses pénitentes'. On one occasion Rimbaud even uses a Latin rather than a French word – 'virides' instead of 'vertes' – to provide the requisite two syllables and a feminine ending and at the same time a rhyme for 'rides'.

In 'Le Bateau ivre' and 'Voyelles' Rimbaud is therefore no longer concerned primarily with 'telling a story' and it may be that the endless arguments about the exact meaning of these two poems spring in a large measure from the fact that the balance between the orderly control of the intellect and the free play of the imagination has shifted towards the latter, without, however, the former being completely abandoned as it had been in the 'nonsense verse' included in the 'lettre du voyant'.

In other poems written in the last half of 1871 the balance seems to have shifted still further towards the ideas expressed in the 'lettre du voyant'. 'L'Orgie parisienne ou Paris se repeuple', for example, which is dated from the same month as the 'lettre du voyant', May 1871, has something of the same quality about it as 'Chant de guerre parisien'. The 'coup d'archet' this time, as the sub-title suggests, and has been mentioned above, is the flooding back into Paris of those who had fled during the troubles of 1871, and from then on the poem is swept along on a series of sarcastic commands from Rimbaud to the returning crowds:

> O lâches, la voilà! Dégorgez dans les gares!
> Le soleil essuya de ses poumons ardents
> Les Boulevards qu'un soir comblèrent les Barbares.
> Voilà la cité sainte, assise à l'occident!
>
> Allez! on préviendra les reflux d'incendie
> Voilà les quais, voilà les boulevards, voilà
> Les maisons sur l'azur léger qui s'irradie
> Et qu'un soir la rougeur des bombes étoila!
>
> Cachez les palais morts dans des niches de planches!
> L'ancien jour effaré rafraîchit vos regards.
> Voici le troupeau roux des tordeuses de hanches:
> Soyez fous, vous serez drôles, étant hagards . . .

At times his torrent of invective seems to take over almost completely so that some of his expressions and some of his rhymes have an awkwardness about them that is strongly reminiscent of 'Chant de guerre parisien':

> O cœurs de saleté, bouches épouvantables,
> Fonctionnez plus forts, bouches de puanteurs!
> Un vin pour ces torpeurs ignobles, sur ces tables . . .
> Vos ventres sont fondus de hontes, ô Vainqueurs!
>
> Ouvrez votre narine aux superbes nausées!
> Trempez de poisons forts les cordes de vos cous!
> Sur vos nuques d'enfants baissant ses mains croisées
> Le poète vous dit: 'O lâches, soyez fous!' . . .

Yet despite the impression that in 'L'Orgie parisienne' Rimbaud is simply allowing his thoughts and feelings to unfold without exercising any control over them, nevertheless, as in 'Le Bateau ivre' though less obviously so, there is a pattern of thought in the poem suggesting that he was not content to play the rôle of an entirely passive instrument.

This can scarcely be said to be the case, however, with another poem written during this period, though at an unspecified date, 'Les Mains de Jeanne-Marie'. Here there seems little doubt that Rimbaud is giving completely free rein to his imagination. The main driving force behind the poem appears to be a desire, if not exactly to parody, at least to re-write, on very different principles, the well-known 'Etude de Mains' published by Théophile Gautier in *Emaux et Camées* in 1852 and the poem entitled 'Tes Mains' in *Les Chimères* in 1866 by Albert Mérat whom Rimbaud names as one of his favourite poets of the 'nouvelle école dite parnassienne' towards the end of the 'lettre du voyant'. But whereas Mérat depicts pale and delicate hands:

> Bien qu'elles soient d'un marbre pâle
> Tes mains fines que j'adorai,
> Et que jamais la dent du hâle
> N'ait pu mordre leur grain nacré . . .

and Gautier sees a woman's hand engaged in romantically feminine activities:

> A-t-elle joué dans les boucles
> Des cheveux lustrés de Don Juan,
> Ou sur son caftan d'escarboucles
> Peigné la barbe du sultan . . . ,

Rimbaud, on the contrary, seems more concerned with the strong brown hands of the women who took part in the Commune, the 'pétroleuses' as they were known because of their capacity for throwing the 1871 equivalent of 'Molotov cocktails'. But this is not to say that the poem consistently and coherently develops this theme; on the contrary, in the very first stanza the third line is in flagrant contradiction with the second line, and the fourth line ends with what is surely a hastily made up rhyme inspired by the reference to Don Juan in the stanza from Gautier's poem quoted above:

> Jeanne-Marie a des mains fortes,
> Mains sombres que l'été tanna,
> Mains pâles comme des mains mortes.
> —Sont-ce des mains de Juana?

The second stanza of Rimbaud's poem, again like the one from Gautier's 'Etudes de mains', is in the form of a question and it introduces the word 'voluptés' used by Gautier in his next stanza:

> Ont-elles pris les crèmes brunes,
> Sur les mares des voluptés?
> Ont-elles trempé dans les lunes
> Aux étangs de sérénités?

But it is difficult to make much sense of these lines and one is tempted to think that the reference to 'lunes' has reminded Rimbaud of one of the lunar seas, the *Mare Serenitatis*, and that he has transformed the first of these Latin words into a French word and used it in the second line, substituting for it the word 'étangs' in association with 'sérénités' in the fourth line. Elsewhere in the poem there is further evidence to suggest that Rimbaud is not exercising any conscious control over his material but is simply letting his thoughts wander round his theme, accepting whatever word suggests itself. The ninth stanza, for instance, is another example of two ideas in apparent conflict being juxtaposed, followed by two lines whose sole purpose appears to be to provide the requisite number of syllables and more or less suitable rhyming words:

> Ce sont des ployeuses d'échines,
> Des mains qui ne font jamais mal,
> Plus fatales que des machines,
> Plus fortes que tout un cheval.

The twelfth stanza too ends with rhyming words that seem to have little else to recommend them and the second line of the stanza simply does not make any kind of sense:

> L'éclat de ces mains amoureuses
> Tourne le crâne des brebis!
> Dans leurs phalanges savoureuses
> Le grand soleil met un rubis!

Nor is this the only poem of the latter part of 1871 in which Rimbaud seems to give full effect to the ideas advanced in the 'lettre du voyant'. On 14 July 1871 he wrote to Théodore de Banville enclosing a fairly lengthy poem of 160 lines divided, like 'Chant de guerre parisien', 'Mes petites amoureuses' and 'Les Mains de Jeanne-Marie', into quatrains of eight syllable lines and entitled 'Ce qu'on dit au poète à propos de fleurs'. Just as 'Les Mains de Jeanne-Marie' mocks the poetry of Gautier and Mérat, so 'Ce qu'on dit au poète . . .' mocks the poetry of Banville who had not deigned to reply to Rimbaud's earlier letter of 24 May 1870[9] and who is now the butt of the latter's sarcasm:

Monsieur et cher Maître,
        Vous rappelez-vous avoir reçu de province, en juin 1870, cent ou cent cinquante hexamètres mythologiques intitulés 'Credo in unam'? Vous fûtes assez bon pour répondre! C'est le même imbécile qui vous envoie les vers ci-dessus, signés Alcide Bava.—Pardon. J'ai dix-huit ans. —J'aimerai toujours les vers de Banville. L'an passé je n'avais que dix-sept ans! Ai-je progressé?

As one would expect, in view of these impertinent remarks to an established poet thirty years his senior, the 'coup d'archet' of the poem is an attack on the poetry of Banville with its surfeit of lilies, roses and lilacs, coupled with a demand for a more vigorous and imaginative kind of poetry:

> En somme, une Fleur, Romarin
> Ou Lys, vive ou morte, vaut-elle
> Un excrément d'oiseau marin?
> Vaut-elle un seul pleur de chandelle? . . .

> Trouve, aux abords du Bois qui dort,
> Les fleurs, pareilles à des mufles,
> D'où bavent des pommades d'or
> Sur les cheveux sombres des Buffles! . . .

Trouve des Chardons cotonneux
Dont dix ânes aux yeux de braises
Travaillent à filer des nœuds!
Trouve des Fleurs qui soient des chaises! . . .

Toi, fais jouer dans nos torpeurs,
Par les parfums les hystéries;
Exalte-nous vers des candeurs
Plus candides que les Maries . . .

Such lines seem to herald certain verses of 'Le Bateau ivre' that Rimbaud was to compose a few weeks later:

J'ai suivi, des mois pleins, pareille aux vacheries
Hystériques, la houle à l'assaut des récifs,
Sans songer que les pieds lumineux des Maries
Pussent forcer le mufle aux Océans poussifs!

J'ai heurté, savez-vous, d'incroyables Florides
Mêlant aux fleurs des yeux de panthères à peaux
D'hommes! Des arcs-en-ciel tendus comme des brides
Sous l'horizon des mers, à de glauques troupeaux! . . .

Glaciers, soleils d'argent, flots nacreux, cieux de braises
Echouages hideux au fond des golfes bruns
Où les serpents géants dévorés des punaises
Choient, des arbres tordus, avec de noirs parfums . . .

Presque île, ballottant sur mes bords les querelles
Et les fientes d'oiseaux clabaudeurs . . .

But although this desire to replace the pedestrian, descriptive verse of Banville and his like by a more exciting and exotic kind of poetry constitutes the general theme of 'Ce qu'on dit au poète . . .', there seems little doubt that, having decided on his theme, Rimbaud simply let his imagination run riot, as careless of conflicting terms, meaningless expressions and nonsensical rhymes as in other poems of the same kind:

Ainsi, toujours, vers l'azur noir
Où tremble la mer des topazes
Fonctionneront dans ton soir
Les Lys, ces clystères d'extases! . . .

Commerçant! colon! médium!
Ta Rime sourdra, rose ou blanche,
Comme un rayon de sodium,
Comme un caoutchouc qui s'épanche!

On more than one occasion he borrows unusual rhymes from the very poet he is attacking, whose virtuosity in this respect was well-known. But whereas Banville's rhymes are carefully integrated into the poem, as in the following couplet from 'Méditation' in *Odes funambulesques*:

> Aujourd'hui Weill possède un bouchon de carafe,
> Arsène a ses maisons, Nadar est photographe,

Rimbaud's borrowings are only loosely linked to the sense of the poem:

> De vos forêts et de vos prés,
> O très paisibles photographes
> La Flore est diverse à peu près
> Comme des bouchons de carafes!

Similarly a stanza from an earlier poem in *Odes funambulesques*, 'La Ville enchantée':

> La Belle au bois dormant, sur la moire fleurie
> De la molle ottomane où rêve le chat Murr,
> Parmi l'air rose et bleu des feux de la féerie
> S'éveille après cent ans sous un baiser d'amour;

is the source of some particularly inconsequential lines in 'Ce qu'on dit au poète . . .':

> Quelqu'un dira le grand Amour,
> Voleur des sombres Indulgences:
> Mais ni Renan, ni le chat Murr
> N'ont vu les Bleus Thyrses immenses,

Stanzas such as these seem to prove beyond doubt that 'Ce qu'on dit au poète . . .' is to be classed along with the poems of the 'lettre du voyant' and 'Les Mains de Jeanne-Marie' as yet another attempt by Rimbaud to abandon conscious control over his material and to let it develop of its own accord. This means that from May to September 1871, to a greater or lesser degree, most of his poems have about them a certain air of 'dérèglement'; he is clearly striving after 'des inventions d'inconnu' and 'des formes nouvelles', even though he has not yet had the boldness to break away from the accepted conventions of rhyme and rhythm. This was to be something he was to learn from Verlaine during the next few months in Paris.

III

THE LATER POETRY: 1871–1872

The manuscripts

Like most of the poetry he had written up to September 1871, the poems Rimbaud wrote during the next twelve months remained in manuscript form for many years. It was not until as late as 1936 that it became known that he had contributed twenty short pieces of verse to the *Album zutique*, a collection of parodies of the work of such notable figures as Banville, Bourget and Coppée by such iconoclasts as Verlaine, Cros and Richepin who, after the demise of an earlier group, known as the *Vilains Bonshommes*, had founded, in 1871, a new group known, for some obscure reason, as the *Cercle zutique*. But precisely because these poems are parodies they are of no great significance except as proof of his facility and versatility as a poet.

Of perhaps rather more importance are three obscene poems that he wrote at about the same time, that is to say towards the end of 1871, known as the *Stupra*, two of which remained unpublished until 1923, although the third, entitled the 'Sonnet du trou du cul', was included in 1902 in Verlaine's posthumous volume of obscene poems, *Hombres*, on the grounds that it was in fact a joint creation by both Verlaine and Rimbaud, the former having composed the quatrains and the latter the tercets. Verlaine indicates that the sonnet is a parody of the work of Albert Mérat, whose poem 'Tes Mains', as has been suggested above, Rimbaud may already have parodied in 'Les Mains de Jeanne-Marie' and who had devoted a whole volume of verse, *L'Idole*, in 1869, to poems about various parts of the body. But the significant point about the sonnet is that it is a celebration of homosexuality in the most detailed terms and it therefore does much to confirm the existence of homosexual relations between Verlaine and Rimbaud. A similar tone is adopted in the second sonnet 'Nos fesses ne sont pas les leurs', while the first sonnet, 'Les anciens animaux saillissaient, même en course' is reminiscent of 'Soleil et chair' and 'Les Premières Communions' in its theme that, in the modern world, sexuality is denied the frank and open rôle that it once played.

Much more significant than either the verses of the *Album zutique* or the three sonnets of the *Stupra* are the other nineteen poems that

Rimbaud wrote during this period, most of which were published
in the magazine *La Vogue* in 1886, thanks to the efforts of Verlaine,
while the remainder appeared in *Le Reliquaire* in 1891 and in subsequent editions of Rimbaud's work, usually under the heading
'derniers vers', although Antoine Adam prefers to call them 'vers
nouveaux et chansons'. Eleven of these poems are dated on the
original manuscripts, seven of them from May 1872 ('Larme', 'La
Rivière de cassis', 'Comédie de la soif', 'Bonne Pensée du matin',
'Bannières de mai', 'Chanson de la plus haute tour' and 'L'Eternité'), two from June 1872 ('Age d'or' and 'Jeune Ménage') and
two from July ('Bruxelles' and 'Est-elle almée'). A twelfth poem,
'Fêtes de la faim', probably belongs to August, although this date
was added by another hand after the poem had been written.
Another half dozen poems are undated ('Mémoire', 'Qu'est-ce
pour nous', 'Honte', 'Michel et Christine', 'O Saisons, ô chateaux'
and 'Entends comme brame') and one poem, 'Le Loup criait', is
assumed to be from this period, although no manuscript exists,
on the grounds that Rimbaud quoted it in *Une Saison en enfer* along
with some of the other poems.

Chronology and meaning

Charleville, late 1871

It may be that one of the undated poems, 'Mémoire', was in fact
written before Rimbaud's departure to join Verlaine in Paris in
September 1871. The setting of the poem is a river, presumably
the Meuse at Charleville, bordered by willow trees and flowing
through meadows surrounded by hills. In the final lines the poet
is reluctantly held fast in a 'canot immobile', unable to grasp the
flowers that lie beyond his reach. He envies the pollen shaken free
from the willow catkins at the slightest touch of a bird's wing and
the heads of the reeds swept away by the current. He himself, in
contrast, is firmly anchored in his boat, stuck in the mud, both
literally and metaphorically:

> Jouet de cet œil d'eau morne, je n'y puis prendre,
> ô canot immobile! oh! bras trop courts! ni l'une
> ni l'autre fleur: ni la jaune qui m'importune,
> là; ni la bleue, amie à l'eau couleur de cendre.
>
> Ah! la poudre des saules qu'une aile secoue!
> Les roses des roseaux dès longtemps dévorées!

> Mon canot, toujours fixe; et sa chaîne tirée
> Au fond de cet œil d'eau sans bords,—à quelle boue?

The similarity between these ideas and those expressed in 'Le
Bateau ivre' is striking; Rimbaud's urgent plea towards the end of
'Le Bateau ivre': 'O que ma quille éclate! O que j'aille à la mer!',
is complementary to the deep discouragement he expresses
towards the end of 'Mémoire' at being held fast in his 'canot
immobile'. Since both poems thus express, through the same symbol of the boat, the same intense longing to escape, explicit in the
one case and implicit in the other, it seems reasonable to conclude
that both were written at about the same time, all the more so
because other factors, of a formal nature, tend to confirm this
dating, as will be shown in the third section of this chapter.

Paris, late 1871

If 'Mémoire' may therefore have been written before Rimbaud's
departure from Charleville to join Verlaine in Paris in September
1871, it is generally agreed that another of the undated poems,
'Qu'est-ce pour nous, mon cœur, que ces nappes de sang', was
written shortly after his arrival in the capital when the sight of the
devastation left by the defeat of the Commune three months before
awakened in him an intense desire for vengeance:

> Qu'est-ce pour nous, mon cœur, que les nappes de sang
> Et de braise, et mille meutres, et les longs cris
> De rage, sanglots de tout enfer renversant
> Tout ordre; et l'Aquilon encore sur les débris
>
> Et toute vengeance? Rien! . . .—Mais si, tout encor,
> Nous la voulons! Industriels, princes, sénats,
> Périssez! puissance, justice, histoire, à bas!
> Ça nous est dû. Le sang! le sang! la flamme d'or!

The last two stanzas of the poem achieve an apocalyptic quality as
Rimbaud extends his destructive rage to encompass the whole
world, even if it means that he and his fellow 'Communards' will
be destroyed in the process, although in a detached final line he
returns from his delirious vision to the harsh reality of life:

> Europe, Asie, Amérique, disparaissez.
> Notre marche vengeresse a tout occupé,
> Cités et campagnes!—Nous serons écrasés!
> Les volcans sauteront! et l'océan frappé . . .

Oh! mes amis!—mon cœur, c'est sûr, ils sont des frères:
Noirs inconnus, si nous allions! allons!
O malheur! je me sens frémir, la vieille terre,
Sur moi de plus en plus à vous! la terre fond,

Ce n'est rien! j'y suis! j'y suis toujours.

A third undated poem, 'Honte', may well have been written not
long afterwards in view of the fact that it has something of the
same feeling of violence and anger, suddenly lapsing into a similar
kind of pathos at the end. But it is very different from 'Qu'est-ce
pour nous . . .' in that it is an entirely personal poem. Rimbaud
has been deeply hurt at having been dismissed as an 'enfant
gêneur', a 'si sotte bête', either by his mother, as some critics have
proposed, or by Verlaine, as other critics have argued. The latter
seems much the more likely suggestion, although Verlaine was no
doubt simply passing on the views of his wife Mathilde and her
family and perhaps too of his literary friends in Paris who had
reacted unfavourably to the upsetting presence among them of
the seventeen-year-old Rimbaud. The theme of the poem is a
simple one – as long as he is alive Rimbaud will constantly have to
resort to trickery – but its simplicity is concealed by the complicated syntax and the curiously naïve yet vivid imagery:

Tant que la lame n'aura   Mais, non, vrai, je crois que tant
Pas coupé cette cervelle,   Que pour sa tête la lame,
Ce paquet blanc, vert et gras   Que les cailloux pour son flanc,
A vapeur jamais nouvelle . . .   Que pour ses boyaux la flamme

N'auront pas agi, l'enfant
Gêneur, la si sotte bête,
Ne doit cesser un instant
De ruser et d'être traître,

Comme un chat des Monts-Rocheux,
D'empuantir toutes sphères . . .[1]

Rimbaud clearly sees himself as a martyr who will ultimately
suffer a painful death and it is this which leads to the pathetic plea
of the last two lines:

Qu'à sa mort pourtant, ô mon Dieu,
S'élève quelque prière!

Something of the childish feeling of self-pity that wells up at the
end of 'Les Chercheuses de poux' can be detected in these lines,

and there is a touch of childishness too in the spiteful and exaggerated malevolence of the second stanza where, in an aside placed in parenthesis, Rimbaud attacks Verlaine:[2]

> (Ah! Lui, devrait couper son
> Nez, sa lèvre, ses oreilles,
> Son ventre! et faire abandon
> De ses jambes, ô merveille!)

The Ardennes, May 1872

All this anger and self-pity disappears, however, from one of the poems bearing the date 'May 1872', 'La Rivière de cassis'. Despite the fact that the word 'cassis' is given a capital initial letter in the manuscript version, although not in the version printed in *La Vogue*, it is generally agreed that Rimbaud is using the word in its colour sense and that, as his friend Ernest Delahaye was the first to suggest, he is referring to the dark and shadowy waters of the Semois, a tributary of the Meuse that winds through a deep valley of the Ardennes north of Charleville. As one might expect from the fact that Rimbaud had returned home towards the end of March 1872 after spending six months in Paris,[3] the theme of the poem is the feeling of renewed vigour that the countryside gives to the poet. 'Que salubre est le vent', he exclaims, somewhat prosaically; more romantically he imagines 'les passions mortes des chevaliers errants', thinking no doubt of Godefroy de Bouillon through whose medieval stronghold the Semois flows, and of the 'rocher des quatre fils Aymon' near its junction with the Meuse. Even the cawing of the crows is transformed into a 'vraie et bonne voix d'anges'. The whole poem, in fact is a fairly straightforward hymn of praise to the countryside, closely related to 'Les Corbeaux' which is usually classed among the poems of 1870–1 although its date is unknown and several critics consider that it was written at the same time as 'La Rivière de cassis'.

Another poem with a country setting bears the enigmatic title 'Michel et Christine' and, although it is undated, there seems little doubt that it too was written in the Ardennes in May 1872. Its opening stanzas could in fact be taken on a realistic level as an account of a gathering storm, with Rimbaud urging a flock of sheep, a sheepdog and a shepherd to seek shelter. But the poem then moves on to a non-realistic plane and it becomes apparent that the shepherd and his sheep are to be taken as symbolic of those who lack the courage and strength to face up to difficulties. Rimbaud, on the contrary, refuses to be counted among them, just as he had refused, at the end of 'Le Bateau ivre', to follow, sheep-like, in the wake of others:

> Mais moi, Seigneur! voici que mon esprit vole,
> Après les cieux glacés de rouge, sous les
> Nuages célestes qui courent et volent
> Sur cent Solognes longues comme un railway.

> Voilà mille loups, mille graines sauvages
> Qu'emporte, non sans aimer les liserons,
> Cette religieuse après-midi d'orage
> Sur l'Europe ancienne où cent hordes iront!

This 'Europe ancienne' clearly echoes the 'Europe aux anciens parapets' of 'Le Bateau ivre', but the transformation of the storm sweeping across Europe into a religious movement and the use of the word 'horde' with its connotation of barbarian invasions suggest that Rimbaud has widened the scope of this particular symbol and that he now regards 'l'Europe ancienne' as the protective yet restrictive stability not just of his own life in Charleville, but of the whole of European civilization which he wishes to see swept away.

The impression that Rimbaud is now extending to others his own personal desire to break free from the confines of traditional European standards ('Il faut que j'en aide d'autres; c'est mon devoir', he was later to say in *Une Saison en enfer*) is continued in the following stanza where the barbarian hordes change, somewhat paradoxically, into a band of medieval crusaders who have fought their way through to a haven of peace and refuge:

> Après, le clair de lune! partout la lande,
> Rougis et leurs fronts aux cieux noirs, les guerriers
> Chevauchent lentement leurs pâles coursiers!
> Les cailloux sonnent sous cette fière bande!

This leads to the decidedly hermetic final stanza where Rimbaud, wondering if he too will reach his promised land, sees the latter in romantic terms as a sunlit valley inhabited by the happy couple of the title, whose names are borrowed from a comedy by Eugène Scribe. But behind these symbols there lies a second layer of

imagery borrowed from Christian sources, although it seems unlikely that Rimbaud could be envisaging a Christian solution to
his problems in view of the ideas so far expressed in his poetry. He
is no doubt using Christian imagery for his own purposes to convey the impression of a new religion by which he hopes to see
Christianity replaced. The final line of the poem in particular
seems to imply this where the name 'Christine' calls to his mind
the name of Christ whose appearance puts an end to the idyllic
picture he has been painting:

> —Et verrai-je le bois jaune et le val clair,
> L'Epouse aux yeux bleus, l'homme au front rouge, ô Gaule,
> Et le blanc agneau Pascal, à leurs pieds chers,
> —Michel et Christine,—et Christ!—fin de l'Idylle.

These lines not only echo those poems of 1871 such as 'Soleil et
chair' and 'Les Premières Communions' which attack Christianity, but they also herald the theme of the first chapter of *Une Saison
en enfer* in which Rimbaud stresses his 'gaulois' ancestry and protests that he is not by nature a Christian.

A third poem with a country setting that was presumably
written in the Ardennes is 'Comédie de la soif', one of the poems
bearing the date 'mai 1872'. It is linked with 'Michel et Christine'
in so far as the thirst of the title is clearly of a symbolic nature and
cannot be assuaged by what is offered to Rimbaud in the opening
stanzas by 'les Grands-Parents, les Grands' – cider and milk, tea
and coffee, 'les liqueurs dans nos armoires' – all of which may also
be symbols caricaturing traditional remedies for the ills of the
human condition. Nor can the poet find any consolation in the
fictitious world of the imagination offered by 'l'Esprit' in the
second section of the poem:

> Légendes ni figures
> Ne me désaltèrent.

Nor is he tempted by the invitation of 'les Amis' in the third
section of the poem to seek a means of escape through 'les Vins',
'le Bitter sauvage' and 'l'Absinthe aux verts piliers'. But despite
his rejection of these proposed solutions to his difficulties, he
remains obsessed, in the fourth section of the poem, 'Le Pauvre
Songe', by his dream of one day finding a haven of peace and
refuge where his thirst will finally be satisfied:

> Peut-être un Soir m'attend
> Où je boirai tranquille
> En quelque vieille Ville
> Et mourrai plus content
> Puisque je suis patient.

He doubts, however, whether any further wanderings such as he had undertaken in 1870 and 1871 can lead him to the place of rest that he is seeking:

> Et si je redeviens
> Le voyageur ancien
> Jamais l'auberge verte
> Ne peut bien m'être ouverte.

Precisely what it is that Rimbaud is thirsting after is never explicitly defined, but the two concluding stanzas of the poem imply that, as in 'Le Bateau ivre', it is an intense longing for freedom which constitutes his 'soif si folle qui mine et désole':

> Les pigeons qui tremblent dans la prairie,
> Le gibier, qui court et qui voit la nuit,
> Les bêtes des eaux, la bête asservie,
> Les derniers papillons! . . . ont soif aussi.
>
> Mais fondre où fond ce nuage sans guide,
> —Oh! favorisé de ce qui est frais!
> Expirer en ces violettes humides
> Dont les aurores chargent ces forêts?

'Bannières de mai' is yet another poem dated 'mai 1872' whose setting suggests that it was written in the Ardennes rather than in Paris. Moreover, it is the first of four poems grouped under the common title of 'Fêtes de la patience' which, like the word 'patient' in 'Comédie de la soif', must surely refer to Rimbaud's weeks of waiting in Charleville. His loneliness and boredom, his longing to be 'moins seul et moins nul' form the theme of 'Bannières de mai' and this theme is continued with even greater urgency in the second of the 'Fêtes de la patience', also dated 'mai 1872' and entitled 'Chanson de la plus haute tour':

> J'ai tant fait patience
> Qu'à jamais j'oublie;
> Craintes et souffrances
> Aux cieux sont parties.
> Et la soif malsaine
> Obscurcit mes veines.

Rimbaud's thirst in these lines (the image is also used in 'Bannières de mai') presumably has the same significance as in 'Comédie de la soif' – the thirst for freedom, the desire to escape once more from Charleville. But it may refer more specifically to a longing to renew the relationship with Verlaine who, in a letter approximately dated 'avril 1872' had written: 'Certes, nous nous reverrons! Quand?—Attendre un peu! Nécessités dures! Opportunités raides!'. The second stanza of the poem certainly appears to refer to Rimbaud's having agreed to leave Paris in order to enable Verlaine and his wife to 'retaper leur ménage', according to the expression used by Verlaine in the letter mentioned above:

> Je me suis dit: laisse,
> Et qu'on ne te voie:
> Et sans la promesse
> De plus hautes joies.
> Que rien ne t'arrête
> Auguste retraite.

The final stanza too, which is a repeat of the first stanza, appears to refer to the sacrifice Rimbaud had made by agreeing to return to Charleville in a moment of weakness or generosity which he now regrets:

> Oisive jeunesse
> A tout asservie,
> Par délicatesse
> J'ai perdu ma vie.
> Ah! Que le temps vienne
> Où les cœurs s'éprennent!

The last two lines are of special interest in that they move from the particular issue of Rimbaud's relationship with Verlaine to the general issue of 'l'amour universel'. The latter expression occurs in Verlaine's 'Crimen amoris' where Rimbaud appears in the guise of 'le plus beau d'entre tous les mauvais anges' who, in order to preach his sermon about the abolition of good and evil, climbs to the topmost tower of an infernal palace:

> Le voyez-vous sur la tour la plus céleste
> Du haut palais avec une torche au poing?

It seems difficult to doubt that Rimbaud's title, 'Chanson de la plus haute tour', is related to these lines and that they in turn confirm that Rimbaud's theme is his particular desire to renew his relationship with Verlaine and his general wish to see all such relationships become an accepted part of life.

Paris, May-June 1872

The third of the 'Fêtes de la patience', also dated 'May 1872' and entitled 'L'Eternité', is one of the most mysterious of the poems of this period. The first three stanzas, like those of 'Michel et Christine', could almost be taken at their face value as a magnificent evocation of the transition from night to day and of the feeling of being above the things of this world that the contemplation of the dawn can give:

> Elle est retrouvée.   Ame sentinelle,
> Quoi?—L'Eternité.   Murmurons l'aveu
> C'est la mer allée   De la nuit si nulle
> Avec le soleil.   Et du jour en feu.
>
> Des humains suffrages,
> Des communs élans
> Là tu te dégages
> Et voles selon.

But since Rimbaud could not have watched the dawn rising over the sea at the time the poem was written, it seems reasonable to suppose that, as in 'Michel et Christine', the imagery is of a symbolic nature. If the probable chronological position of the poem is then borne in mind and the general sense of the poems so far discussed, the opening lines could well have the very obvious meaning that the eternity that has been rediscovered is the renewed relationship with Verlaine on the occasion of Rimbaud's return to Paris towards the end of May 1872.[4] It is worth noting, in this connection, that in one of the passages of the *Illuminations*, 'Matinée d'ivresse', echoing, or heralding, the ideas expressed in Verlaine's 'Crimen amoris' mentioned above, Rimbaud was to write:

> ... On nous a promis d'enterrer dans l'ombre l'arbre du bien et du mal, de déporter les honnêtetés tyranniques afin que nous amenions notre très pur amour. Cela commença par quelques dégoûts et cela finit,—ne pouvant nous saisir sur le champ de cette éternité,—cela finit par une débandade de parfums.

Not only is the term 'éternité' thus used to describe the emotiona experience shared with Verlaine, but it is worth noting too Rimbaud's often quoted claim in another of the *Illuminations*, 'Vagabonds', that he had undertaken to restore Verlaine to his 'état primitif de fils du soleil' which further suggests what the symbolic significance of the imagery in 'L'Eternité' may be.

The remainder of the poem confirms in some measure that the imagery is meant to be understood symbolically, in that, again as in 'Michel et Christine', religious overtones creep into the poem as Rimbaud reflects on the duty that this new dawn in his life imposes on him; and again he seems to look beyond his particular relationship with Verlaine to his long-term mission of spreading the gospel of 'l'amour universel' more widely. But he is well aware that he has no hope of ever completing such a task, that he will never be acclaimed as a new prophet and that a long, patient and painful struggle is all that awaits him:

> Puisque de vous seules, Là pas d'espérance,
> Braises de satin, Nul orietur.
> Le devoir s'exhale Science avec patience
> Sans qu'on dise: enfin. Le supplice est sûr.

These lines seem to be echoed twelve months later in *Une Saison en enfer*, both in 'Mauvais sang', where Rimbaud protests that 'je n'ai jamais été chrétien; je suis de la race qui chantait dans le supplice', and in the chapters 'L'Impossible' and 'L'Eclair' where he complains that 'la science ne va pas assez vite pour nous' and that 'la science est trop lente'.

The suggestion that 'L'Eternité' was written after Rimbaud had left Charleville towards the end of May is supported by the fact that the fourth and last of the 'Fêtes de la patience', 'Age d'or', is dated 'Juin 1872' when he was definitely back in Paris. There is also some connection between the titles 'L'Eternité' and 'Age d'or' in that both imply an entry into a kind of paradise, but otherwise the two poems are markedly different. 'Age d'or' is clearly an unfinished piece of work and it bears all the signs of having been hastily dashed off, rather in the manner of the doggerel verse of the 'lettre du voyant'. Lines and stanzas are repeated for no apparent reason; the indication 'etc.' is added at the end of several stanzas, again for no apparent reason; a six syllable line occurs in the fourth stanza of what is otherwise a poem in five syllable lines; the last two stanzas are of five lines whereas all the other stanzas are quatrains; and in general there is a disjointed, incoherent effect to the poem, as is obvious from the following typical stanzas:

Reconnais ce tour
Si gai, si facile:
Ce n'est qu'onde, flore,
Et c'est ta famille!

Puis elle chante. O
Si gai, si facile,
Et visible à l'œil nu . . .
—Je chante avec elle,—

Reconnais ce tour
Si gai, si facile,
Ce n'est qu'onde, flore,
Et c'est ta famille! . . . etc . . .

But beneath the incoherence can be perceived, in two of the stanzas, Rimbaud's disquiet about where his ideas were leading him:

Ces mille questions
Qui se ramifient
N'amènent, au fond,
Qu'ivresse et folie . . .

Le monde est vicieux;
Si cela t'étonne!
Vis et laisse au feu
L'obscure infortune.

Although 'Age d'or' is dated, as has been said, 'Juin 1872' and ends the cycle of the 'Fêtes de la patience', there are two other poems dated from May 1872 which do not form part of the cycle and yet which may well have been written immediately after Rimbaud's return to Paris towards the end of May and therefore just before 'Age d'or'.

The first of these is 'Bonne Pensée du matin' which has very much the same atmosphere of calm resolution as 'L'Eternité' with nothing of the anxious, questioning note of 'Michel et Christine', 'Comédie de la soif', 'Bannières de mai' and 'Chanson de la plus haute tour'. As with 'L'Eternité', if the poem is read bearing in mind the circumstances of Rimbaud's life in May 1872, it could simply be taken as referring to the renewal of the relationship with Verlaine in Paris at the end of that month:

A quatre heures du matin, l'été,
Le sommeil d'amour dure encore.
Sous les bosquets l'aube évapore
L'odeur du soir fêté.

It is interesting in this connection to note that, in the letter to Delahaye from Paris headed 'Juinphe 1872' Rimbaud writes:

Le mois passé ma chambre, rue Monsieur-le-Prince, donnait sur un jardin du lycée Saint-Louis. Il y avait des arbres énormes sous ma fenêtre étroite. A trois heures du matin la bougie pâlit . . .

A later passage in the same letter reads:

A cinq heures je descendais à l'achat de quelque pain; c'est l'heure. Les ouvriers sont en marche partout . . . Le premier matin en été . . . voilà ce qui m'a ravi toujours ici.

This could well be the setting of the second and third stanzas of 'Bonne pensée du matin':

> Mais là-bas dans l'immense chantier
> Vers le soleil des Hespérides,
> En bras de chemise, les charpentiers
>   Déjà s'agitent.
>
> Dans leur désert de mousse, tranquilles,
> Ils préparent les lambris précieux
> Où la richesse de la ville
>   Rira sous de faux cieux.

Difficult though it is to understand the two particular expressions 'soleil des Hespérides'[5] and 'désert de mousse'[6] these stanzas as a whole could clearly refer simply to the extensive rebuilding that was going on in Paris at the time. This could also explain the allusion, in the fourth verse, to 'Babylone' since the term is, or was in Rimbaud's day, often used as a synonym for a wealthy city:

> Ah! pour ces Ouvriers charmants
> Sujets d'un roi de Babylone,
> Vénus! laisse un peu les Amants,
>   Dont l'âme est en couronne.

The planet Venus is commonly known as the 'étoile du berger' and this no doubt explains the reference in the first line of the last verse to the 'Reine des Bergers', although the mention of the sea in the final line is more enigmatic unless, as has been suggested,[7] this is a playful pun on 'l'amer' or what Rimbaud had called, in 'Comédie de la soif', 'le bitter sauvage':

> O Reine des Bergers!
> Porte aux travailleurs l'eau-de-vie,
> Pour que leurs forces soient en paix
>   En attendant le bain dans la mer, à midi.

If one moves away from this literal reading of the poem to look for a metaphorical meaning it is difficult to find a satisfactory explanation, although a recent critic has argued that the poem is concerned with poetry rather than with life and that the first stanza is a rejection of the kind of love poetry Verlaine had written in *La Bonne Chanson*, in place of which Rimbaud then proposes an imaginative, creative, visionary kind of poetry symbolized by such words as 'chantier', 'charpentiers' and 'ouvriers' thus heralding the fantasy townscapes that later figure in the *Illuminations*.[8]

The last of the poems dated 'May 1872' seems to express a disenchantment with Paris and, correspondingly, offers a nostalgic picture of life in Charleville. 'Les rivières ardennaises et belges, voilà ce que je regrette', wrote Rimbaud in his letter from Paris in 'Juinphe 1872', and it is this feeling of regret for the previous weeks spent in the countryside round Charleville that forms the opening theme of 'Larme':

> Loin des oiseaux, des troupeaux, des villageoises,
> Je buvais, accroupi dans quelque bruyère
> Entouré de tendres bois de noisetiers,
> Par un brouillard d'après-midi tiède et vert.
>
> Que pouvais-je boire dans cette jeune Oise,
> Ormeaux sans voix, gazon sans fleurs, ciel couvert.

Thus far the poem is a realistic recollection of an afternoon spent in solitude on the banks of the Aisne which flows close to the Rimbaud farm at Roche on its way to join the Oise at Compiègne. The next two lines, however, suddenly move on to what can only be a symbolic level:

> Que tirais-je à la gourde de colocase?
> Quelque liqueur d'or, fade et qui fait suer.

The drinking vessel, as exotic as it is unrealistic (a 'colocase' is an edible plant, not a tree from which wooden bowls can be made) and the mysterious golden potion that paradoxically acts like a poison surely indicate that Rimbaud is endowing the life he had led in the Ardennes with a deeper significance, the nature of which is suggested by the contrast between the idea of something precious implied in the expression 'liqueur d'or' and the idea of something unpleasant implied in the words 'fade et qui fait suer'. For although Rimbaud may have regretted the 'rivières ardennaises et belges', at the same time he had been glad to leave them behind, just as in 'Le Bateau ivre' he had both welcomed 'l'Europe aux anciens parapets' as a place of shelter and rejected it as a place of imprisonment. It seems therefore that in these two strange lines

Rimbaud is simply saying once again that life at home in the Ardennes had been both precious to him and at the same time unbearably insipid.

In the third stanza, after wryly admitting that he would have been no great advertisement for the 'liqueur d'or':

> Tel, j'eusse été mauvaise enseigne d'auberge,

Rimbaud introduces a sudden change of tense:

> Puis l'orage changea le ciel jusqu'au soir,
> Ce furent des pays noirs, des lacs, des perches,
> Des colonnades sous la nuit bleue, des gares . . .

There seems little doubt that these lines must refer to Rimbaud's return to Paris towards the end of May and that he is using the word 'orage' in a symbolic sense – the darkening of his horizon as he plunged once more into the troubled relationship with Verlaine. The river flowing through the woods then became no more than a memory and the warm pools of the Ardennes faded from his mind:

> L'eau des bois se perdait sur des sables vierges.
> Le vent, du ciel, jetait des glaçons aux mares . . .

This brings us to the two enigmatic final lines:

> Or! tel qu'un pêcheur d'or ou de coquillages,
> Dire que je n'ai pas eu souci de boire!

Again it is important to note the precise tense that is used in the last line and to bear in mind that 'n'avoir pas souci de' means 'not to bother to do something'. Rimbaud is therefore exclaiming with astonishment that he had not bothered to drink from his 'gourde de colocase', that he had not paid attention to the 'liqueur d'or'. And the reason why he had not done so was because, like a pearl diver or a man in search of gold, he was looking for some particular kind of treasure, not realizing that the riches he was seeking were all round him.

In other words 'Larme', as the title indicates, is a poem of regret; its theme is like that of 'Le Bateau ivre' but in reverse; in 'Le Bateau ivre', having tasted the heady delights of freedom, Rimbaud could no longer bear to remain within the confines of 'l'Europe aux anciens parapets'; in 'Larme', on the contrary, he recognizes that, although he had not realized it at the time, it was

in the peace and quiet of the Ardennes, to which he had returned
in the spring of 1872, that the Eldorado he was seeking was to be
found.

A similar sense of sadness and sorrow at having failed to reach
an ideal pervades the undated poem 'O saisons, ô châteaux' which
is even more obscure in its meaning than 'Larme'. The opening
line alone has given rise to a variety of interpretations, but if one
assumes that the poem was written in Paris along with 'L'Eternité',
'Bonne Pensée du matin' and 'Larme' towards the end of May
1872, then this sigh of regret could clearly refer to the castles
mentioned in 'La Rivière de cassis' that Rimbaud has left behind
and to the countryside of the Ardennes where he could have
appreciated the passing seasons of the year so much more than in
Paris. The second line too would fit in with this interpretation and
with the theme of 'Larme' in that it implies, if somewhat elliptically, that Rimbaud wonders whether he has been at fault in
abandoning the tranquillity of country life:

> O saisons, ô châteaux,
> Quelle âme est sans défauts?

The reason why he has done so is given in the next couplet which
echoes his symbolic pursuit of gold and pearls in 'Larme' and the
self-imposed duty to which he had referred in 'l'Eternité':

> J'ai fait la magique étude
> Du Bonheur que nul n'élude.

The third couplet sings the praises of this pursuit of happiness:

> O vive lui, chaque fois
> Que chante le coq gaulois.

The second of these two lines would appear at first sight to be no
more than a periphrasis for 'chaque matin', but the word 'gaulois',
as has been mentioned above, is one that Rimbaud was to use in
the opening chapter of *Une Saison en enfer* to indicate his pre-
Christian attitude to life and it may be therefore that the use of
the same adjective in 'O saisons, ô châteaux' suggests that he is
looking for happiness outside the sphere of Christian morals and
beliefs. It is to be noted too that, when the poem is quoted at the
end of 'Délires II' in *Une Saison en enfer*, it is immediately preceded
by the following passage:

Le Bonheur! Sa dent, douce à la mort, m'avertissait au chant du coq,
—*ad matutinum*, au *Christus venit*,—dans les plus sombres villes.

This seems to be a veiled allusion to Saint Peter's denial of Christ at cock crow and would seem to suggest therefore that Rimbaud denied his Christian upbringing in order to pursue his quest for happiness.

Certain critics, however, reject these Biblical allusions and prefer to see in the line: 'Que chante le coq gaulois' what Antoine Adam calls 'un sens gaillard' since this expression is used in the Ardennes area to describe sexual desire. In support of this interpretation Adam quotes an earlier variant of the couplet:

> Je suis à lui chaque fois
> Que chante son coq gaulois,

but he is surely at fault to assume that these two interpretations are incompatible, for it is precisely because of his desire for happiness that Rimbaud has engaged in his homosexual relationship with Verlaine contrary to Christian teaching.

The fourth couplet emphasizes that he no longer has any feelings of envy for others happier than himself; his life has been completely invaded by happiness; or perhaps by Verlaine if one prefers to interpret in this way the pronoun at the beginning of the second line of the couplet:

> Mais l je n'aurais plus d'envie,
> Il s'est chargé de ma vie.

This pronoun in the third person may in fact have yet a third meaning if one links it with the opening noun of the fifth couplet:

> Ce Charme! il prit âme et corps
> Et dispersa tous efforts.

All three of these meanings are of course, closely related and Rimbaud may well be deliberately fusing them in order to convey the fascination that Verlaine had for him and the happiness that resulted, at least temporarily, from their relationship. As for the last part of the first line of the fifth couplet, once again there is a connection with *Une Saison en enfer* which ends with Rimbaud's declaration, after his break with Verlaine, that he is no longer going to be dependent on others and that henceforth: 'Il me sera loisible de *posséder la vérité dans une âme et un corps*'. It seems reasonable to suppose that this is an echo of the line 'O saisons, ô châteaux' and that it is therefore Verlaine who has taken him over body and soul and consumed all his energy.

It is for this reason, according to the sixth couplet, that his poetry has lost its clarity and vigour:

> Que comprendre à ma parole?
> Il fait qu'elle fuie et vole.

There seems little doubt that the second of these two lines is an allusion to the kind of poetry that Verlaine was then practising and that he was to preach in his 'Art poétique' two years later:

> Que ton vers soit la chose envolée
> Qu'on sent qui fuit d'une âme en allée
> Vers d'autres cieux à d'autres amours.

It is on this note that the poem ends, but the manuscript version adds two further couplets which Rimbaud crossed out. It may be that he discarded these seventh and eighth couplets because their vocabulary is such that they clearly refer to a particular person, presumably Verlaine, and they come close to depriving the poem of that aura of mystery and ambiguity which makes it so fascinating:

> Et si le malheur m'entraîne
> Sa disgrâce m'est certaine.
>
> Il faut que son dédain, las!
> Me livre au plus prompt trépas!

The reference to 'sa disgrâce' must clearly mean Verlaine's disfavour which Rimbaud would earn if he were to abandon his search for happiness and return to his old unhappy existence. Similarly the words: 'son dédain' in the final couplet must refer to Verlaine's disdain which Rimbaud would find unbearable.

This enigmatic and haunting little poem is unusual in that it is perhaps the only occasion when Rimbaud appears to be dominated by Verlaine instead of being much the more powerful personality of the two. But, to be strictly accurate, it is the narrator in the poem who is dominated by the other person involved, and it may be that this narrator is in fact intended to be Verlaine to whom, in the chapter 'Délires I' of *Une Saison en enfer*, Rimbaud attributes words reminiscent of those in 'O saisons, ô châteaux':

Ses délicatesses mystérieuses m'avaient séduite. J'ai oublié tout mon devoir humain pour le suivre . . . Hélas, je dépendais bien de lui.

Mais que voulait-il avec mon existence terne et lâche? . . . Tristement dépitée je lui dis quelquefois: 'Je te comprends'. Il haussait les épaules . . . Je me pressentais, lui parti, en proie au vertige, précipitée dans l'ombre la plus affreuse: la mort.

If 'O saisons, ô châteaux' shares with the three poems dated 'mai 1872', 'L'Eternité', 'Bonne pensée du matin' and 'Larme', a note of sadness, 'Jeune Ménage', which is precisely dated '27 juin 1872', resembles 'Age d'or', written in the same month, in that Rimbaud has recovered from his feeling of despondency. It has been suggested that the title may refer to Verlaine and his wife Mathilde and that the poem is a caricature of the picture of wedded bliss that Verlaine had over-optimistically conjured up in *La Bonne Chanson*. But it seems much more likely, as other critics have suggested, that the title refers to what is described at the end of 'Délires I' in *Une Saison en enfer* as the 'drôle de ménage' – that is the relationship between Verlaine and Rimbaud. The poem is set in a single room, such as the one in the Hôtel de Cluny from which Rimbaud wrote his letter headed 'juinphe 1872' that has been mentioned above. Moreover, the opening lines suggest the untidiness and lack of space typical of rooms of this sort:

> La chambre est ouverte au ciel bleu-turquin;
> Pas de place: des coffrets et des huches!

and the beginning of the second stanza seems an obvious allusion to Verlaine's efforts to find somewhere for Rimbaud to stay in Paris:

> Que ce sont bien intrigues de génie
> Cette dépense et ces désordres vains!

It is worth noting too that Verlaine was to include in *Jadis et Naguère* a poem on a similar subject, 'Le Poète et la muse', in which he recalled one of the rooms that he and Rimbaud had lived in during the latter's first few months in Paris in 1872:

> La chambre, as-tu gardé leurs spectres ridicules
> O pleine de jour sale et de bruits d'araignées.[9]

This was the period when Verlaine, whose recent marriage was on the verge of collapse, was spending more time with his 'époux infernal' than with his 'épouse légitime' and this could explain the reference, in the fourth stanza of 'Jeune Ménage' to the 'absence ici, tout le temps' of 'le jeune marié'. Similarly, the 'malin rat' of the fifth stanza, who interrupts the honeymoon of the 'jeune ménage', could well be a slighting reference to Mathilde whom Verlaine was to address as 'princesse souris' in a letter he wrote to her a month later when she made a final vain attempt to break up the increasingly intimate relationship between the two poets who had set off together for Belgium on 7 July.[10]

But although one can thus try to identify certain figures from the world of reality in the poem, certain other figures appear who are clearly figments of Rimbaud's vivid imagination. It is in the last two lines of the first stanza that the reader is led into this world of fantasy:

> Dehors le mur est plein d'aristoloches
> Où vibrent les gencives des lutins.

Why goblins' gums should vibrate among the climbing plant known as aristolochia which covers the wall outside has, not surprisingly, puzzled generations of commentators and critics, unaware perhaps that aristolochia is commonly known as 'Dutchman's pipe' because of the curious shape of the flowers and that Rimbaud may therefore have imagined these floral pipes set in the mouths of goblins hidden away among the leaves. The last two lines of the second stanza allude to another fantasy creature who has provided a blackberry bush or mulberry bush (the word 'mûre' can mean either) and 'des résilles' (which can mean either 'lattice work' or 'hairnet'):

> C'est la fée africaine qui fournit
> La mûre, et les résilles dans les coins.

Again one can only guess as to what basis in reality this African fairy might have – a chambermaid or the hotel proprietor might be two possibilities – and why she should have provided such different and ambiguous items. The third stanza contains an equally curious allusion to the entry of several 'discontented godmothers' who, even more curiously, slip into the sideboards like patches of light:

> Plusieurs entrent, marraines mécontentes,
> En pans de lumière dans les buffets.

They are accompanied, in the last two lines of the fourth stanza, by water sprites drifting round the room:

> Même des esprits des eaux, malfaisants,
> Entrent vaguer aux sphères de l'alcôve.

Finally, in the last stanza, Rimbaud appeals for a will-o'-the-wisp to appear in the evening, or failing that, for some angelic figures to watch over the 'jeune ménage':

> —S'il n'arrive pas un feu follet blême,
> Comme un coup de fusil après les vêpres.
> —O spectres saints et blancs de Bethléem,
> Charmez plutôt le bleu de leur fenêtre.

Belgium, July-August 1872

The period that Rimbaud and Verlaine spent in Belgium in July and August 1872 is reflected in the poem entitled 'Bruxelles' and headed 'Juillet. Boulevard du Régent'. But it is far from being a realistic description along the lines of the 'simples fresques' set in the Belgian capital that Verlaine was writing at the same time and that he was to include in *Romances sans paroles*. On the contrary, Rimbaud's poem plunges the reader into an even more disordered and incoherent world than in 'Jeune Ménage':

> Plates-bandes d'amaranthe jusqu'à
> L'agréable palais de Jupiter
> —Je sais que c'est Toi qui, dans ces lieux,
> Mêles ton Bleu presque de Sahara!

This is reminiscent of the inconsequential imagery of the poems enclosed in the 'lettre du voyant' more than twelve months before and the final line of the second stanza is in fact filled out with meaningless sounds similar to the 'abracadabrantesques' of 'Le Cœur supplicié':

> Puis, comme rose et sapin du soleil
> Et liane ont ici leurs jeux enclos,
> Cage de la petite veuve! . . .
> > > > > > Quelles
> Troupes d'oiseaux, ô ia io, ia io!

The third stanza is full of equally inconsequential and obscure allusions:

> Calmes maisons, anciennes passions!
> Kiosque de la Folle par affection.
> Après les fesses des rosiers, balcon
> Ombreux et très bas de la Juliette.

It has been suggested that the 'Folle par affection' is Shakespeare's Ophelia and that, continuing in the same vein, Juliette is another of his heroines, but nobody has yet succeeded in identifying the railway station called 'Henriette' to which Rimbaud refers in the next stanza:

> —La Juliette, ça rappelle l'Henriette,
> Charmante station du chemin de fer.

It looks therefore as if Rimbaud is again trying his hand at the same kind of nonsense verse as in the 'lettre du voyant' with Brussels as the 'coup d'archet' initially inspiring the poem which is then built up of a series of unexplained allusions and impressions noted down without any effort to shape them into a coherent whole, although an unsuccessful attempt is made to round off the poem by an extraordinarily prosaic final stanza:

> —Boulevard sans mouvement ni commerce,
> Muet, tout drame et toute comédie,
> Réunion des scènes infinie,
> Je te connais et t'admire en silence.

The same kind of illogicality and banality characterizes the two curious stanzas, also dated 'juillet 1872', in which Rimbaud wonders, in the first, whether an unidentified 'elle', as mysterious as the 'toi' of the previous poem, is an Egyptian dancer[11] who will disappear at dawn like a faded flower against the splendid backcloth of Brussels:

> Est-elle almée? . . . aux premières heures bleues
> Se détruira-t-elle comme les fleurs feues . . .
> Devant la splendide étendue où l'on sente
> Souffler la ville énormément florissante!

The second stanza appears to be totally unconnected with the first and to be an even more enigmatic mixture of unidentified figures and mysterious settings introduced by an oddly detached line whose total lack of any poetic quality is even more marked than that of the last line of the preceding stanza:

> C'est trop beau! c'est trop beau! mais c'est nécessaire
> —Pour la Pêcheuse et la chanson du Corsaire,
> Et aussi puisque les derniers masques crurent
> Encore aux fêtes de nuit sur la mer pure!

'Fêtes de la faim', probably written in August 1872,[12] continues in this vein of unexplained allusions, curious images and meaningless sounds that Rimbaud seems now to have adopted:

> Ma faim, Anne, Anne,
> Fuis sur ton âne.
>
> Si j'ai du *goût*, ce n'est guères
> Que pour la terre et les pierres.
> Dinn! dinn! dinn! dinn! Mangeons l'air,
> Le roc, les charbons, le fer.[13]

The two remaining poems of 1872, 'Entends comme brame' and 'Le loup criait' are undated but the fact that both of them have, to a marked degree, the incoherence of 'Bruxelles', 'Est-elle almée' and 'Ma faim, Anne, Anne', suggests that they too date from the summer of 1872. C. A. Hackett believes that 'Entends comme brame' may have been initially inspired by a desire on Rimbaud's part to caricature Verlaine's poetry and in particular the poem 'La lune blanche' in *La Bonne Chanson*.[14] It is certainly true that Rimbaud's references to:

> la brume qu'exhale   and   . . . ce brouillard triste
> ce nocturne effet,   et blémi, justement,

are reminiscent not only of 'La lune blanche' and other poems in *La Bonne Chanson* but also of several poems in *Romances sans paroles* such as 'L'ombre des arbres dans la rivière embrumée' and 'Dans l'interminable Ennui de la plaine'. But it is equally true that 'Entends comme brame' makes no attempt at a skilful or subtle parody but simply takes a typically Verlainian five syllable rhythm, adds some of his notoriously weak rhymes, borrows some of his characteristically misty imagery and loosely links these elements together, along with whatever material comes to mind, to make up nonsense verses similar to those in the 'lettre du voyant':

> Entends comme brame   Loin des claires meules
> près des acacias   des caps, des beaux toits,
> en avril la rame   ces chers Anciens veulent
> viride du pois!   ce philtre sournois . . .
>
> Dans sa vapeur nette,   Or ni fériale
> vers Phœbe! tu vois   ni astrale! n'est
> s'agiter la tête   la brume qu'exhale
> de saints d'autrefois . . .   ce nocturne effet.

Néanmoins ils restent,
— Sicile, Allemagne
dans ce brouillard triste
et blémi, justement!

As for 'Le loup criait', this too is clearly a series of 'coq-à-l'âne', not unlike 'Entends comme brame' except that on this occasion there is no intention of caricaturing Verlaine:

Le loup criait sous les feuilles   Les salades, les fruits
En crachant les belles plumes   N'attendent que la cueillette;
De son repas de volailles: Mais l'araignée de la haie
Comme lui je me consume.   Ne mange que des violettes.

Que je dorme! que je bouille
Aux autels de Salomon.
Le bouillon court sur la rouille,
Et se mêle au Cédron.

The second stanza in particular has an inconsequential note that is reminiscent of 'Chant de guerre parisien' and 'Mes petites amoureuses', especially the last two lines which are as devoid of sense as the lines from the latter discussed above:

On mangeait des œufs à la coq
Et du mouron.

The third stanza too, with its conflicting verbs in the first line, recalls the element of contradiction in two lines from 'Les mains de Jeanne-Marie':

Ce sont des ployeuses d'échines
Des mains qui ne font jamais mal.

As for the obvious play on the sound '-ouille' in the third verse, this echoes the similar play on the sound 'a' in the opening line of 'Mes petites amoureuses':

Un hydrolat lacrymal lave
Les cieux vert-chou.

The poems of late 1871 and 1872 seem therefore, like those enclosed in the 'lettres du voyant' and those written between May and September 1871, to be a mixture of poems with a serious purpose and poems which can fairly be described as nonsense verse. If the chronology that has been suggested in the preceding pages is correct it would even appear that the nonsense verse is broadly

limited to the last half dozen poems when Rimbaud had set off for
Belgium with Verlaine and when, removed from the stresses and
strains of life in Paris or Charleville, he may have felt in a more
light-hearted mood.

Towards freedom of form

But although there are therefore similarities of tone between the
poetry dating from the middle of 1871 and the poetry dating from
late 1871 and 1872, there is a decided difference between them as
regards their versification. For it was in the poems of late 1871 and
1872, no doubt as a result of the liberating influence of Verlaine,
that Rimbaud loosened the bonds of rhyme and rhythm by which
he had until then been so severely restricted. It may even be
possible to trace his increasing boldness in this respect as he
adopted certain of Verlaine's techniques and then went beyond
them to a greater freedom of form than anything Verlaine had
ever attempted or, indeed, ever would attempt.

It is interesting to note, in this connection, that the first of any
of Rimbaud's poems to break with the orthodox canons of versification is the sonnet 'Voyelles', written in the summer of 1871. Like
'Mandoline' in Verlaine's *Fêtes galantes* (a volume for which
Rimbaud had expressed his admiration in a letter to his teacher
Izambard dated 25 August 1870) it is in feminine rhymes throughout, with the exception of the single masculine rhyme 'studieux' and
'yeux' in the tercets. It may therefore be significant that 'Mémoire'
too abandons the alternation of masculine and feminine rhymes in
favour of feminine rhymes throughout and that 'Qu'est-ce pour
nous' which, as has been mentioned above, is generally agreed to
date from September 1871, also abandons the conventional alternation of masculine and feminine rhymes, this time in favour of
successive masculine rhymes, like 'En Sourdine' in *Fêtes galantes*.
But apart from the introduction of this modest Verlainian inno-
vation these two poems are perfectly orthodox and are in fact the
only poems among the later poetry to be written, like most of the
earlier poetry, in alexandrines. This lends additional support to
the suggestion made above that 'Mémoire' may date from before
Rimbaud's departure for Paris in September 1871 and to the
generally accepted opinion that 'Qu'est-ce pour nous' dates from
immediately after his arrival in the capital.[15]

It has also been suggested above that 'Honte' may have been

written towards the end of 1871 or early in 1872 when Rimbaud's relationship with Verlaine was becoming increasingly difficult for the latter's family and friends to tolerate. In this case too the mildly audacious form of the poem lends support to this view. Although it reverts to the alternation of masculine and feminine rhymes, it is the first of Rimbaud's poems to use an 'impair' rhythm and, moreover, a typically Verlainian one of seven syllables such as the latter had used in both 'Mandoline' and 'En Sourdine'. But 'Honte' also ventures the introduction of two further irregularities of a kind that Verlaine had never dared to risk – a slightly incorrect rhyme between 'bête' and 'traître' in the penultimate stanza and a slightly out-of-step rhythm of eight instead of seven syllables in the penultimate line.

'La Rivière de cassis', which as has been shown above may have been the first to be written of the poems dated May 1872, is an amalgam, as far as its technique is concerned, of the three previous poems. It resembles 'Mémoire' in that the rhymes are exclusively feminine in the first stanza; it resembles 'Qu'est-ce pour nous' in that the rhymes are exclusively masculine in the second stanza; and it resembles 'Honte' in that it reverts to the traditional alternation of masculine and feminine rhymes in the third stanza. It further resembles 'Honte' in that there is a slightly incorrect rhyme between 'anges' and 'plongent' in the first stanza, but it extends freedom of form a little further by the use of a false rhyme in the third stanza between 'envoie' and 'matois', heralding Verlaine's poem 'C'est le chien de Jean de Nivelle' in *Romances sans paroles* which is entirely made up of such 'rimes fausses'. The rhythms too, in 'La Rivière de cassis', seem to be the work of a poet experimenting more and more with new forms. Like 'Honte' it is in 'vers impairs', but this time of eleven and five syllables in the first stanza and eleven and seven syllables in the second and third stanzas, which means that Rimbaud has again gone beyond Verlaine in that, although the latter had used five and seven syllable lines, he had never used the eleven syllable line and was not to do so until 'Il faut, voyez-vous, nous pardonner les choses' in *Romances sans paroles*.

A second poem written in eleven syllable lines is the undated 'Michel et Christine' which, it has been suggested above, may have been composed shortly after 'La Rivière de cassis'. Once again the versification seems to lend support to this view in that, as in 'Honte' and 'La Rivière de cassis', there is an incorrect rhyme in the first stanza between 'bords' and 'honneur'. But in the second stanza Rimbaud goes even further and instead of pairing two words which are not too far apart phonetically, as has always been the case so far, he abandons all semblance of rhyme with the words 'amaigries' and 'orage'. Similarly in the final stanza he 'rhymes' 'Gaule' and 'Idylle', although one could argue in this case that there is some link between the two words in the alliteration of the final consonant.

'Comédie de la soif' also betrays a certain restiveness with rhyme in the pairing of 'rares' and 'fleurs' in the third stanza and 'piliers' and 'amis' in the third section of the poem. But it is the rhythm that is particularly worthy of note in that Rimbaud experiments with an even greater variety of lengths of line than in 'La Rivière de cassis'; the poem begins with three stanzas of seven syllable lines, except for the second line in each stanza which is of two syllables; then comes a group of four quatrains with lines of five and six syllables alternately; the third section of the poem is divided into six lines of six syllables and six lines of five syllables; the three stanzas of the fourth section are in six syllable lines; and finally the two quatrains forming the concluding section are in decasyllabic lines.

If 'Comédie de la soif' seems to be trying to break away from uniform rhythm, 'Bannières de mai' seems like a deliberate exercise in the progressive abandoning of rhyme. The first stanza preserves tenuous links between the 'rhyming' words by means of alliteration and assonance – 'tilleuls' and 'hallali', 'spirituelles' and 'groseilles', 'veines' and 'vignes', 'comme un ange' and 'communient', 'blesse' and 'mousse'; the second stanza moves still further away from true rhyme – 'ennuie' and 'peines', 'dramatique' and 'fortune', 'nature' and 'meure', 'drôle' and 'monde'; whilst the third stanza moves completely into the field of blank verse, with not the slightest trace of any similarity of sound between the words which end each line – 'm'usent' and 'rends', 'soif' and 'abreuve', 'illusionne' and 'soleil', 'rien' and 'infortune'. But as if to compensate for these audacities Rimbaud decorously returns to the octosyllabic rhythm that he had used on a number of occasions in his early poetry.

With the three poems which, it has been suggested above, Rimbaud wrote when he was about to return or had just returned to Paris towards the end of May 1872, there is a temporary retreat from the adventurousness of the previous few poems. All three of them are in the Verlainian rhythm of 'vers impairs' of five syllables, perhaps because Verlaine was uppermost in Rimbaud's mind at that time. The first of them, 'Chanson de la plus haute tour', has no irregularities of any kind except that it is in feminine rhymes throughout, again suggesting a strong Verlainian influence. The second of the three, 'L'Eternité', returns to the conventional alternation of masculine and feminine rhymes, but it still strikes a modest blow for freedom of form by replacing true rhymes on three occasions by words that are linked merely by assonance or alliteration – 'éternité' and 'soleil', 'sentinelle' and 'nulle', 'seules' and 's'exhale'. The third poem, 'Age d'or', also returns to the alternation of masculine and feminine rhymes but it too uses approximate rhymes on half a dozen occasions between 'tour' and 'flore', 'facile' and 'famille', 'o' and 'nu', 'facile' and 'elle', 'étonne' and 'infortune', 'château' and 'es-tu'.

'Age d'or' also slips in an irregular line of six syllables in the fourth stanza, just as 'Honte' had slipped an eight syllable line into a poem which is otherwise in lines of seven syllables. But it is in 'Bonne pensée du matin', dated May 1872 and no doubt written towards the end of that month, that Rimbaud totally abandons uniformity of rhythm with lines of twelve, ten, nine, eight, six and four syllables arranged in a quite random pattern, although the rhyme scheme, as if to provide a firm anchorage for this highly irregular rhythm, is entirely conventional save for the slightly incorrect rhyme between 'Hespérides' and 's'agitent'.

The reverse is true of what is probably the next poem, 'Larme', since here the lines are of eleven syllables throughout, but the majority of the rhymes are irregular – 'villageoises' and 'noisetiers', 'bruyère' and 'vert', 'couvert' and 'suer', 'auberge' and 'perches', 'vierges' and 'coquillages' – although there is clearly some degree of assonance and alliteration between these pairs of words so that there is not the complete abandoning of rhyme that is such a feature of the final stanza of 'Bannières de mai'.

By this stage Rimbaud seems to have reached the limit of his experimentation with verse forms and the remaining poems of 1872 are fairly conventional, although not entirely so. 'O saisons, ô châteaux' is in rhyming couplets of seven syllable lines apart from the first couplet which is in six syllable lines with the opening line being repeated as the third line and again as the final line. Despite these irregularities the poem is so Verlainian in tone that, as has been suggested above, it seems possible that it may be meant as a Verlaine pastiche, reminiscent of 'O triste, triste était mon âme' in *Romances sans paroles* which is in octosyllabic rhyming couplets. It has also been suggested above that 'Entends comme brame' may be meant as a Verlaine parody with its quatrains in 'vers impairs' of five syllables, although it strays slightly further from the path of conventional versification by introducing two incorrect rhymes between 'restent' and 'triste' and between 'Allemagne' and 'tristement' into the final stanza and by ending with a line that has one syllable too many. 'Le loup criait', on the other hand, has two lines that have one syllable too few among its three quatrains of seven syllable lines and it also has two incorrect rhymes between 'feuilles' and 'volailles' and between 'fruits' and 'haie'. 'Jeune Ménage' and 'Bruxelles' resemble each other in that both have a decasyllabic rhythm, although 'Bruxelles' slips in three lines of nine syllables in the first, second and third stanzas, and both poems make do with a number of incorrect rhymes – 'huches' and 'aristoloches', 'floue' and 'alcôve', 'blême' and 'Bethléem', 'vêpres' and 'fenêtre' in 'Jeune Ménage'; 'Jupiter' and 'lieux', 'soleil' and 'quelles', 'balcon' and 'Juliette', 'Henriette' and 'verger', 'commerce' and 'silence' in 'Bruxelles'. Finally the two quatrains of 'Est-elle almée' with their eleven syllable lines and feminine rhymes throughout are Verlainian in technique if not in tone, as are the opening and closing couplets and the intervening five quatrains of four and seven syllable lines that make up 'Fêtes de la faim', although Verlaine would never have condoned Rimbaud's rhyming of 'déluges' and 'grises' and 'noir' and 'tire'.

Despite these experiments with greater freedom of form, Rimbaud still remains bound on occasions by the kind of constraints that, before September 1871, he had never dared to flout and there are several examples in the 'vers nouveaux' of rhymes which, like so many of those in 'Chant de guerre parisien', 'Mes petites amoureuses' and other poems written between May and September 1871, have obviously sprung to his mind purely and simply because they are rhyming words and have promptly been used regardless of their meaning. In the second stanza of 'Le loup criait', for example, it seems certain that the word 'violettes' has been inserted merely because it offers an easy rhyme with 'cueillette' although it is nonsense to talk of spiders eating violets. Similarly, in 'Entends comme brame', the word 'rame' is completely meaningless in association with the verb 'bramer' (a technical term used to describe the bellowing of a stag in the mating season) and is clearly there simply to provide a rhyme, just as the function of the word 'avril' is to provide two syllables to make up a five syllable line rather than to indicate the time of the year when peasticks (which is what the word 'rame' means here) are to be seen supporting growing peas. Such peasticks would not, in any case, merit the adjective 'virides', although Rimbaud no doubt remembered having already created this word, modelled on the Latin 'viridis', in the sonnet 'Voyelles'. 'Bruxelles' is another poem which offers an interesting example of Rimbaud's occasional reluctance to dispense with rhyme; the term 'bleu de Sahara' in the fourth line of the first stanza does not make sense, but Rimbaud needed a rhyme for 'jusqu'à' and it may be that he had in mind a poem that Verlaine wrote at about the same time, 'Malines' in *Romances sans paroles*, which refers to the

> . . . château de quelque échevin
> Rouge de brique et bleu d'ardoise,

and in the following stanza describes the flat Belgian countryside as a 'Sahara de prairies'; Rimbaud may therefore have casually juxtaposed words borrowed from his fellow-poet so as to make up the rhyme and rhythm he required. Even in one of the more serious poems of 1872, 'Larme', the word 'colocase', completely meaningless in that particular context, presumably sprang into Rimbaud's mind for purely phonetic reasons as a way of providing both the necessary number of syllables and at the same time an adequate rhyme for 'Oise'.

On the whole however, in the poetry of late 1871 and 1872 Rimbaud has moved some distance away from rigid patterns of rhyme and rhythm. The purpose behind this move must surely be to put belatedly into practice the principles towards which he had been feeling his way in the 'lettre du voyant' in his search for 'des formes nouvelles' better able to allow him simply to 'assister à l'éclosion de sa pensée' without having to force his ideas into conventional moulds. The next step for Rimbaud to take was to abandon entirely both rhyme and rhythm and to move into the field of prose poetry so that he could give still freer rein to the 'désordre de son esprit' without letting it be hampered by even the loosened bonds of versification of the poetry written in late 1871 and 1872.

IV

THE *ILLUMINATIONS*: 1872–?

The problem of dates

The problem of the date of composition of the forty-two short passages, most of them in prose, but some of them in free verse, which make up the *Illuminations* is one with which numerous critics have grappled for many long years without having yet reached a final solution. Thirty-seven of these passages were published in *La Vogue* in 1886, at the same time as most of the 'vers nouveaux', and the remaining five were published in the *Poésies complètes* of 1895. But, unlike the 'vers nouveaux', not a single one of any of the passages of the *Illuminations* is dated, so other evidence has had to be sought in order to try and establish when they were written.

As has been shown, Rimbaud was clearly moving away from formal verse in 1872 and it is only to be expected that he should then have turned towards free verse and prose poetry. So it is not surprising that as early as November 1872, in a letter from Verlaine to his friend Edmond Lepelletier, there should be a reference to letters from Rimbaud 'contenant des vers et des poèmes en prose' which had been left behind in Paris when the two poets had set off for Belgium on 7 July 1872. In the following year Rimbaud himself, in the postscript of a letter to Delahaye dating from May 1873, referred to 'quelques fragments en prose de moi' that were in Verlaine's hands and that had presumably been written during the months the two poets had spent together in London before separating on their return to France in April 1873. Two years later, in a letter to Delahaye dated 1 May 1875, Verlaine mentions as having in his possession a number of 'poèmes en prose' by Rimbaud which had probably been written before July 1873 when Verlaine's prison sentence, which had lasted until shortly before the letter to Delahaye, had put an end to his close contact with Rimbaud.[1] Finally, in August 1878 the title *Illuminations* was used for the first time in a letter from Verlaine to his brother-in-law, Charles de Sivry: 'Avoir relu *Illuminations* (painted plates) du sieur que tu sais, ainsi que sa *Saison en enfer*'.

Whether these *Illuminations* are the same as the prose poems mentioned in the earlier letters is a matter of conjecture, but it is

nevertheless a reasonable assumption that was generally accepted
as being correct until 1949 when Henri de Bouillane de Lacoste
launched the idea that the *Illuminations* were in fact written in
1874, not in 1872–3, that is to say that they date from after, rather
than before, *Une Saison en enfer* and that the latter is not therefore
Rimbaud's farewell to literature as it had been thought to be. The
evidence for this new dating was of a largely graphological nature
and has since been discredited,[2] but the way was thus opened for
other critics to try and date some or all of the *Illuminations* from
1874, or even later, for a variety of reasons of a biographical,
stylistic or linguistic nature. The present position is that no one
would now deny that at least some of the *Illuminations* date from
1872–3, but there is disagreement about when they were completed. One or two critics, such as Antoine Adam[3] and D. de
Graaf,[4] wish to extend the period of composition as far as 1878;
many more, notably Suzanne Bernard,[5] Marcel Ruff,[6] Enid
Starkie,[7] V. P. Underwood [8] and N. Osmond,[9] set the time limit
at the end of 1874 or the beginning of 1875; and a few, such as
Rolland de Renéville and Jules Mouquet,[10] C. A. Hackett[11] and
the present author,[12] believe that all the *Illuminations* were written
in 1872–3, before *Une Saison en enfer*.

There can clearly be no question of even trying to summarize,
in the limited space available here, all the complex and conflicting
arguments that have been advanced on this issue, although particular points that have been made with regard to certain passages
will be mentioned in the following pages. There is, however, one
general point that should be made: as regards both form and content there is no doubt that the *Illuminations* are precisely what one
would have expected Rimbaud to write during the period between
the 'vers nouveaux' of 1872 and *Une Saison en enfer* in 1873. As will
be shown later in this chapter, the movement away from verse
towards prose is continued, the desire to see the world destroyed
is even stronger than in 'Qu'est-ce pour nous, mon cœur' and in
'Michel et Christine', the parallel desire to find or to create
another world is reminiscent of 'Comédie de la soif', the theme of a
new kind of love echoes 'Chanson de la plus haute tour' and
'L'Eternité', two close companions figure in a number of passages,
as they do in several of the 'vers nouveaux', and the disillusionment of 'Larme' that was to rise to its climax in *Une Saison en enfer*
can be perceived on occasions. But if the date of composition of
the *Illuminations* is extended beyond 1873 one has to assume that

Rimbaud must have returned to the kind of life, the kind of ideas and the kind of writing that he had practised in 1872–3 and that he had dismissed in *Une Saison en enfer*. One has further to assume that, since Rimbaud undoubtedly did, in the end, change his way of life, abandon his ideas and give up writing, he must have gone through a second 'saison en enfer' of which he has left no record. It is, of course, not impossible that the same cycle of experience should have occurred twice within the space of a couple of years, but, on balance, it seems unlikely.

There is a second difficulty, related to the problem of the date of composition, that has to be faced when approaching the study of the *Illuminations*, namely the order in which the passages should be read. Until very recently it was generally assumed that the first thirty-seven passages had been arranged in random fashion in *La Vogue* in 1886, as their editor, Félix Fénéon, maintained, and as is suggested by the fact that, when published in volume form in the same year by the same editor, the order of the poems was completely altered. It was similarly assumed that the order of the remaining five passages in the *Poésies complètes* of 1895 was equally random. But in the introduction to his edition of the *Illuminations* forming the companion volume to the present study, N. Osmond emphasizes the point that many of the passages flow over from one sheet to the next on Rimbaud's original manuscript, so that within these sequences the order cannot be arbitrary. Furthermore, although the order of the sequences themselves may be arbitrary, Osmond is inclined to believe that this is not the case and that when they were first published the passages were therefore in an order which had been decided by their author.[13]

This does not necessarily mean, however, that the order of the passages is of any significance. In none of Verlaine's volumes of verse, to take an obvious example, are the poems set out in a particularly significant order, either chronological or thematic, and it may well be that, if it was indeed Rimbaud who fixed the order of the passages, he followed the example of the elder poet, and perhaps his own preference for 'le dérèglement' and 'le désordre', in arranging them in random fashion. There is certainly no immediately obvious pattern in the way in which the passages follow one another in the *Vogue* edition and although Osmond divides them into seven groups he acknowledges that these 'do not constitute water-tight categories' and that there is 'some overlapping'.[14] In this chapter, therefore, so as to try and give as clear a picture as possible of the meaning of the *Illuminations*, the passages will be grouped according to themes, irrespective of their place in the *Vogue* edition or in any subsequent editions.

Principal themes

Destruction

A spirit of revolt against the world around him forms, as has been shown, one of the constant themes of Rimbaud's earlier poetry and it is not therefore surprising that this same theme is to be found in several of the *Illuminations*. The first of the passages in the *Vogue* edition, 'Après le déluge', paints a chaotic and disenchanted picture of life after the flood, as the dubious virtues of civilization – street-stalls and boats, abattoirs and circuses, cathedrals and hotels – spread across the earth until, in the penultimate paragraph, echoing the 'clair déluge' and the 'éclairs supérieurs' of the storm which sweeps across 'l'Europe ancienne' in 'Michel et Christine', Rimbaud appeals for a second flood to come and sweep everything away:

> —Sourds, étang,—Ecume, roule sur le pont et par-dessus les bois;
> draps noirs et orgues, — éclairs et tonnerre, — montez et roulez;
> — Eaux et tristesses, montez et relevez les Déluges . . .

In the final paragraph, 'Soleil et chair', in which Rimbaud regrets the passing of the days when man lived close to nature, may also be echoed as he regrets the subsiding of the flood, the boredom of life since then and man's ignorance of the primitive rituals which seem to be symbolized by a mysterious reference to a witch refusing to reveal her secrets:

> Car depuis qu'ils se sont dissipés . . . c'est un ennui! et la Reine, la
> Sorcière qui allume sa braise dans le pot de terre, ne voudra jamais
> nous raconter ce qu'elle sait et que nous ignorons.

'Soir historique' is a second passage which refers to the horrors of modern civilization, contrasting them with the pleasures of country life and of the imagination in which it is possible to seek refuge. The 'touriste naïf, retiré de nos horreurs économiques', who watches in fear as the barbarian hordes stream past ('Il frissonne au passage des chasses et des hordes') seems to be the equivalent of the shepherd and his sheep who were urged to seek refuge from the gathering storm in 'Michel et Christine' while Rimbaud himself joined the invading forces. But the cataclysm foreseen in the final paragraph of 'Soir historique' is far more devastating than the one in 'Michel et Christine' and is indeed on a cosmic scale which even exceeds the flood of 'Après le déluge' as Rimbaud sees the earth heat up, the seas rise, volcanoes erupt and the whole planet sweep out of orbit so that life is finally exterminated.

'Démocratie' deals with the same theme of destruction, but this time the rôles are reversed and it is modern civilization which is launching a campaign against the primitive world.[15] The tone of the passage is clearly meant to be ironic in its use of the highly pejorative term 'immonde', meaning 'obscene' or 'filthy', to describe a country to which prostitution, mass murder and industrialization are about to be brought in the name of democracy. There is irony too in the idea of a primitive culture, symbolized by the word 'tambour', being destroyed by the no less primitive dialect of the soldiers, and in the fact that the whole of the passage is in inverted commas and is spoken by a colonial soldier well aware of the true nature of the 'civilization' that he and his fellow conscripts will be bringing, distinguished as they are by their brutality, ignorance, barbarity and readiness to destroy the world.

'Conte' also deals with the theme of destruction and, as in the case of 'Soir historique', there is some slight link with 'Michel et Christine' in that the passage is dominated, if not by a barbarian horde, at least by a barbarian prince who tries in vain to destroy everything around him, in an attempt to achieve a kind of ecstasy and a sense of renewal:

> Peut-on s'extasier dans la destruction, se rajeunir par la cruauté! . . .

There is an echo too in these lines of the celebrated paragraph in the 'lettre du voyant':

Le Poète se fait *voyant* par un long, immense et raisonné *dérèglement* de *tous les sens*. Toutes les formes d'amour, de souffrance, de folie . . . il devient entre tous le grand malade, le grand criminel, le grand maudit . . .

The sadistic prince of 'Conte' would seem therefore to be the same person as the 'poète maudit' of the 'lettre du voyant', that is to say Rimbaud himself, and this is further confirmed by the way in which both the prince and the poet resemble the 'époux infernal' in *Une Saison en enfer* of whom the 'vierge folle' says in 'Délires I':

> Je l'écoute faisant de l'infamie une gloire, de la cruauté un charme.

'*Le nouvel amour*'

The destructive mania of the prince is not, however, the only theme of 'Conte'. There is a second theme in that the reason for the prince's all-consuming rage is that, like Rimbaud in the 'lettre du voyant', he is looking for new forms of love:

> Il prévoyait d'étonnantes révolutions de l'amour, et soupçonnait ses femmes de pouvoir mieux que cette complaisance agrémentée de ciel et de luxe. Il voulait voir la vérité, l'heure du désir et de la satisfaction essentiels.

Here too there is a connection with 'Délires I' in *Une Saison en enfer* in which the 'époux infernal' declares:

> . . . Je n'aime pas les femmes. L'amour est à réinventer, on le sait. Elles ne peuvent plus que vouloir une position assurée.

There is also a connection with the first stanza of 'Les Sœurs de charité' in that the 'Génie inconnu' of this earlier poem appears towards the end of 'Conte':

> Un soir il galopait fièrement. Un Génie apparut, d'une beauté ineffable, inavouable même. De sa physionomie et de son maintien ressortait la promesse d'un amour multiple et complexe! d'un bonheur indicible, insupportable même! Le Prince et le Génie s'anéantirent probablement dans la santé essentielle. Comment n'auraient-ils pas pu en mourir? Ensemble donc ils moururent.

There is some dispute as to the identity of this 'Génie' but it is perhaps significant that there are a number of echoes of Verlaine's *Fêtes galantes* in the passage quoted. 'Colloque sentimental', for instance, contains a line from which Rimbaud has borrowed the second half: 'Ah! les beaux jours de bonheur indicible', and 'Les Indolents' uses the term 'mourir' in the same sense as it is used in 'Conte', that is as a euphemism for 'faire l'amour':

> Mourons ensemble voulez-vous?
> . . . Mourons
> Comme dans les Décamérons.

This particular meaning given to the word 'mourir' is emphasized by the use of the word 'décéder', in the true sense of 'mourir', in the final lines of 'Conte' where Rimbaud returns to his oriental allegory and sees the prince dying at the usual age, realizing that the figure he had encountered had not, after all, satisfied his 'désir essentiel' and had not equalled the 'Génie' of his imagination:

> Mais ce Prince décéda, dans son palais, à un âge ordinaire. Le Prince était le Génie. Le Génie était le Prince.
> La musique savante manque à notre désir.

The sense of disappointment and dissatisfaction in the final line is reminiscent of a similar feeling which, it has been suggested, emerges from 'L'Eternité', 'Age d'or' and 'Larme', as it also does from the uneasy relationship between the 'époux infernal' and the 'vierge folle' in *Un Saison en enfer*:

> . . . Tristement dépitée je lui dis quelquefois: 'Je te comprends'. Il haussait les épaules . . . Je lui faisais promettre qu'il ne me lâcherait pas. Il l'a faite vingt fois, cette promesse d'amant. C'était aussi frivole que moi lui disant: 'Je te comprends'.

Another passage in the *Illuminations* which combines the themes of destruction and 'le nouvel amour' is 'Génie' which has further links with 'Conte' by its very title and by the fact that it is a sustained portrait of the 'Génie' who appears briefly at the end of 'Conte'. But it seems doubtful whether the 'Génie' can this time be partly identified with Verlaine; it is much more a portrait of Rimbaud himself, especially in the third paragraph where the wholesale condemnation of the world around him is far more characteristic of the 'époux infernal' than of the 'vierge folle':

> Et nous nous le rappelons et il voyage . . . Et si l'Adoration s'en va, sonne, sa promesse sonne: 'Arrière ces superstitions, ces anciens corps, ces ménages et ces âges. C'est cette époque-ci qui a sombré!'

The remainder of the passage is a magnificent panegyric of this dominating figure whose divine stature is emphasized in the superb final paragraph as he leads humanity forward towards another world:

> Il nous a connus tous et nous a tous aimés. Sachons, cette nuit d'hiver, de cap en cap, du pôle tumultueux au château, de la foule à la plage, de regards en regards, forces et sentiments las, le héler et le voir, et le renvoyer, et sous les marées et au haut des déserts de neige, suivre ses vues, ses souffles, son corps, son jour.

There may well be an echo in these lines of the third stanza from 'L'Eternité':

> Des humains suffrages
> Des communs élans
> Là tu te dégages
> Et voles selon.

In *Une Saison en enfer* too Rimbaud refers, in 'Délires I', to the mission to which he feels he is called:

> ... Il faudra que je m'en aille très loin un jour. Puis il faut que j'en aide d'autres: c'est mon devoir.

And at the end of 'Délires I' the 'vierge folle' visualizes the 'époux infernal' ascending into heaven:

> Un jour peut-être il disparaîtra merveilleusement; mais il faut que je sache, s'il doit remonter à un ciel, que je voie un peu l'assomption de mon petit ami!

This messianic note (to use Suzanne Bernard's term) which characterizes 'Génie' is not present to quite the same degree in 'Départ', but, as the title suggests, there is the same idea of a departure towards another world, even if this time it is of a less elevated nature:

> Assez vu. La vision s'est rencontrée à tous les airs.
> Assez eu. Rumeurs des villes, le soir, et au soleil et toujours.
> Assez connu. Les arrêts de la vie.—O Rumeurs et Visions!
> Départ dans l'affection et le bruit neufs!

In view of the final line there is an obvious temptation to see 'Départ' as a reference to the departure of Rimbaud and Verlaine from Paris for Belgium on 7 July 1872, since none of the other numerous departures in Rimbaud's life to which Antoine Adam draws attention,[16] can fairly be described in quite the same terms. Furthermore, the free verse form of the passage, with rhyming elements at the beginning of the first three lines, supports the suggestion of an early dating.

There is a similar temptation to see 'Mouvement', which is also set out in free verse, as a reference to the next departure of the two poets from Ostend for Dover on 4 September 1872 since the passage is concerned with a ship setting sail, carrying on board among its passengers 'un couple de jeunesse' who are described as 'les conquérants du monde ... chassés dans l'extase harmonique et l'héroïsme de la découverte'. The ship, moreover, is described as an 'ark' set amidst 'la lumière diluvienne', which further suggests the creation of a new world and links 'Mouvement' with 'Après le déluge'.

'A une Raison' too belongs to the category of poems in which Rimbaud wants to change the world and to escape to a new kind of life and a new kind of love. The title appears to be borrowed from the second paragraph of 'Génie':

> Il est l'amour, mesure parfaite et réinventée, raison merveilleuse et imprévue,

and the passage as a whole has the same kind of fervour which can also be detected in 'Solde' where the 'sauts d'harmonie inouïs' offered for sale recall the 'nouvelle harmonie' of 'A une Raison' and where certain lines in particular have the almost delirious quality of the later paragraphs of 'Génie':

> A vendre les Corps sans prix, hors de toute race, de tout monde, de tout sexe, de toute descendance . . .
> Elan insensé et infini aux splendeurs invisibles, aux délices insensibles . . .
> A vendre les Corps, les voix, l'immense opulence inquestionable, ce qu'on ne vendra jamais! Les vendeurs ne sont pas à bout de solde! Les voyageurs n'ont pas a rendre leur commission de si tôt!

The last two sentences clearly imply a recovery of optimism after a period of pessimism and N. Osmond suggests that 'Solde' may therefore celebrate Rimbaud's new relationship with Germain Nouveau in 1874.[17] But it must be remembered that the Rimbaud-Verlaine relationship went through repeated cycles of separation and reconciliation and that Rimbaud must have thought on more than one occasion that his new ideas had failed, only to return to them with renewed vigour. Towards the end of May 1873, for example, after having separated from Verlaine in April and begun *Une Saison en enfer*, Rimbaud rejoined his 'compagnon d'enfer' and returned to London, so that this could well have been an appropriate moment for him to reaffirm that 'les voyageurs ne sont pas à bout de solde'. Another appropriate moment would have been July 1872 when Verlaine and Rimbaud set off on their travels together for the first time. It is interesting in this connection to note that Verlaine's poem 'Walcourt' in *Romances sans paroles*, written in July 1872, ends with the following stanza:

> Gares prochaines,
> Gais chemins grands . . .
> Quelles aubaines,
> Bons juifs errants,

and that the opening phrase of Rimbaud's 'Solde' reads almost like a response to the final line:

> A vendre ce que les Juifs n'ont pas vendu . . .

'Matinée d'ivresse', as the title implies, also adopts a tone of almost delirious fervour, using a vocabulary similar to that of 'Génie' and 'A une Raison'. The 'new harmony' to which Rimbaud looks forward in the opening sentence of 'A une Raison' is contrasted with 'l'ancienne inharmonie' in the first paragraph of 'Matinée d'ivresse' where the promise which rang out in the third paragraph of 'Génie' is also echoed:

> . . . rassemblons fervemment cette promesse surhumaine faite à notre corps et à notre âme créés: cette promesse, cette démence! . . . On nous a promis d'enterrer dans l'ombre l'arbre du bien et du mal, de déporter les honnêtetés tyranniques, afin que nous amenions notre très pur amour.

This 'très pur amour' is clearly the 'nouvel amour' of 'A une Raison' and the 'amour, mesure parfaite et réinventée' of 'Génie', with all three expressions being related to the statement of the 'époux infernal' in *Une Saison en enfer* that has already been quoted:

> Je n'aime pas les femmes. L'amour est à réinventer, on le sait.

It should be added that there is a further relationship, outside Rimbaud's work, with Verlaine's 'Crimen amoris' in which, as has been mentioned earlier, Rimbaud, under the guise of 'le plus beau d'entre tous les mauvais anges', sacrifices the distinction between good and evil to the spreading of the new gospel of 'l'amour universel'.

'Matinée d'ivresse' is, however, unusual among the other passages of the *Illuminations* dealing with 'le nouvel amour' in that at times it is strongly reminiscent of the 'lettre du voyant'. The very title echoes the 'dérèglement de tous les sens' advocated in the letter and the declaration, towards the end of 'Matinée d'ivresse': 'Nous t'affirmons, méthode', is a reminder that it was to be a '*raisonné* dérèglement'. 'Nous avons foi au poison', Rimbaud continues in 'Matinée d'ivresse', and this too is a reminder that in the 'lettre du voyant' of 15 May 1871 he had said of the 'poète voyant': 'Il épuise en lui tous les poisons. . . Ineffable torture où il a besoin de toute la foi'. This notion of a torture which the 'poète voyant' must undergo is also repeated in 'Matinée d'ivresse': 'Ce poison va rester dans toutes nos veines même quand, la fanfare tournant, nous serons rendus à l'ancienne inharmonie. O maintenant, nous, si digne de ces tortures'. Finally the desire of the 'poète voyant' to subject himself to 'toutes les formes d'amour' seems to be related to the desire expressed in 'Matinée d'ivresse' to engage in a love beyond good and evil.

Yet despite these indications that 'Matinée d'ivresse' is concerned with Rimbaud's reaction to his relationship with Verlaine, there are many critics who take the title literally and see the passage as partly or wholly inspired by the drugs which Rimbaud is reputed to have taken. This view is based largely on an etymological interpretation of the final line of the passage: 'Voici le temps des *Assassins*', since the word 'assassin' derives from the Arabic 'haschischin'. But this ignores the fact that the term, or at least its verbal form 'assassiner', is used elsewhere in 'Conte' in the normal sense and also the fact that a wildly destructive rage, as has been shown, is a frequent feature of the *Illuminations* and indeed of Rimbaud's poetry in general, reflecting a fundamental trait in his character rather than any artificially stimulated mood. There seems therefore no need to see 'Matinée d'ivresse' as a drug-induced paean of praise in favour of haschisch when it is perfectly comprehensible and very much in line with other poems as a renewed expression of Rimbaud's intense desire to destroy the world and to rebuild it on the new moral basis of 'l'amour universel'. Nor is there any need to suggest that Rimbaud's lack of experience in drug-taking explains the combination of distaste and elation which characterizes 'Matinée d'ivresse', especially in the conflicting terms used at the beginning of the passage – 'fanfare atroce' and 'chevalet féerique' – and in the last sentence of the first paragraph: 'Cela commença par quelques dégoûts et cela finit—ne pouvant nous saisir sur-le-champ de cette éternité, – cela finit par une débandade de parfums'. As early as May 1871, in the 'lettre du voyant', he had laid stress on the idea of passing through a period of suffering so as to attain ultimate bliss and in 'Michel et Christine' and other poems of 1872 the same theme is present. A not dissimilar mixture of feelings also emerges from

'Conte', reflecting the fact that the relationship between Rimbaud and Verlaine was by no means one of untroubled harmony.

This is equally the case with the first of the three separate passages under the collective title 'Veillées' which is a superbly direct evocation of a moment of not quite perfect bliss between two lovers:

> C'est le repos éclairé, ni fièvre, ni langueur, sur le
> lit ou sur le pré.
> C'est l'ami ni ardent ni faible. L'ami.
> C'est l'aimée ni tourmentante ni tourmentée. L'aimée.
> L'air et le monde point cherchés. La vie.
> —Etait-ce donc ceci?
> —Et le rêve fraîchit.

It is true that these two lovers are not actually identified and it is equally true that this is entirely irrelevant to the appreciation of this marvellous little poem, but it is nevertheless worth making the comparison between it and the opening lines of the first of Verlaine's 'Ariettes oubliées' in *Romances sans paroles* which are remarkably similar, not only in subject matter, but also in vocabulary and syntax:

> C'est l'extase langoureuse,
> C'est la fatigue amoureuse,
> C'est tous les frissons des bois
> Parmi l'étreinte des brises . . .

It is in the last two lines of Rimbaud's poem that the touch of sadness present in the first paragraph of 'Matinée d'ivresse' and in the final line of 'Conte' makes itself felt, just as it does, more explicitly, in the last stanza of Verlaine's poem:

> Cette âme qui se lamente
> En cette plainte dormante
> C'est la nôtre, n'est-ce pas?
> La mienne, dis, et la tienne,
> Dont s'exhale l'humble antienne
> Par ce tiède soir tout bas?

Since Verlaine's poem was first published in *La Renaissance littéraire et artistique* on 18 May 1872 and had presumably been written towards the end of March before Rimbaud left Paris for Charleville,[18] it seems reasonable to suppose that Rimbaud's poem must have been written at about the same time. If this is the case, it must be one of the first of the *Illuminations*, a hypothesis which is supported by the free verse form of the poem, on which further comment will be made in the third section of this chapter.

'Royauté' is another passage which may well have the relationship between Rimbaud and Verlaine as its subject. Again the two figures are not specifically identified, but the fact that one of them is a much more powerful personality than the other and is trying to raise his hesitant partner to the same status as himself[19] echoes the words of the 'vierge folle' in *Une Saison en enfer*: 'Par instants j'oublie la pitié où je suis tombée: lui me rendra forte'. There is also an implicit note of sadness in the final paragraph of 'Royauté' where a threefold use of the past definite tense suggests that the couple's moment of triumph, like the moment of perfect harmony in 'Veillées I' and the 'exquise mort'[20] of 'Conte', is now over:

> En effet ils furent rois toute une matinée où les tentures carminées se relevèrent sur les maisons, et toute l'après-midi, où ils s'avancèrent du côté des jardins de palmes.

This hint of sadness turns to downright impatience in the final lines of 'Ouvriers':

> Non! nous ne passerons pas l'été dans cet avare pays où nous ne serons jamais que des orphelins fiancés. Je veux que ce bras durci ne traîne plus *une chère image*.

As always, the dominant male figure and the subordinate female figure are not specifically identified,[21] but once again the chapter 'Délires I' in *Une Saison en enfer* reveals a similar relationship between the 'vierge folle' and the 'époux infernal', expressed through a not dissimilar vocabulary:

> . . . Je nous voyais comme deux bons enfants, libres de se promener dans le Paradis de tristesse . . . Il disait: 'Comme ça te paraîtra drôle quand je n'y serai plus . . . parce qu'il faudra que je m'en aille très loin un jour. Puis il faut que j'en aide d'autres: c'est mon devoir. Quoique ce ne soit guère ragoûtant . . ., chère âme . . .'

This equivocal relationship is even more markedly ambiguous in the group of eight short passages collectively entitled 'Phrases'. One of them expresses, through a series of fairy-like images, the notion of a flawlessly ecstatic happiness:

> J'ai tendu des cordes de clocher à clocher; des guirlandes de fenêtre à fenêtre; des chaînes d'or d'étoile à étoile, et je danse.

Yet another one, describing what could well be the Belgian countryside through which Verlaine and Rimbaud roamed in July 1872, ends on a mysterious, questioning note, as if their escape from Paris had not, after all, brought the sense of innocence and the quasi-religious experience that had been hoped:

> Une matinée couverte, en Juillet. Un goût de cendres vole dans l'air;—une odeur de bois suant dans l'âtre,—les fleurs rouies—le saccage des promenades,—la bruine des canaux par les champs—pourquoi pas déjà les joujoux et l'encens?

A third passage seems to suggest a sense of alienation from the rest of the world which merely serves to strengthen the bond between the lovers:

> Quand nous sommes très forts,—qui recule? très gais,—qui tombe de ridicule? Quand nous sommes très méchants,—que ferait-on de nous.
> Parez-vous, dansez, riez. Je ne pourrai jamais envoyer l'Amour par la fenêtre.

Yet a fourth passage sounds a note of profound pessimism with the two lovers clinging to each other merely out of despair:

> —Ma camarade, mendiante, enfant monstre! comme ça t'est égal, ces malheureuses et ces manœuvres, et mes embarras. Attache-toi à nous avec ta voix impossible, ta voix! unique flatteur de ce vil désespoir.

A fifth passage begins, in contrast, on a note of calmness and confidence:

> Quand le monde sera réduit en un seul bois noir pour nos quatre yeux étonnés,—en une plage pour deux enfants fidèles,[22]—en une maison musicale pour notre claire sympathie,—je vous trouverai.
> Qu'il n'y ait ici-bas qu'un vieillard seul, calme et beau, entouré d'un 'luxe inoui',—et je suis à vos genoux . . .

Yet the passage abruptly changes and it ends with one of the hitherto loving couple killing the other as a typically Rimbaldian streak of cruelty suddenly emerges:

> Que j'aie réalisé tous vos souvenirs,—que je sois celle qui sait vous garrotter,—je vous étoufferai.

Re-creation

Although five of the passages of 'Phrases' are thus devoted to the problems that Rimbaud faced in trying to escape into a new kind of life through 'le nouvel amour', the three remaining passages are concerned with his parallel desire to escape into the world of the imagination in which he had sought refuge so frequently in his earlier poetry. This desire is clearly expressed in one of the three passages where Rimbaud vividly describes the sensation of sleep overcoming him as he turns down the light, flings himself on the bed and sees in the darkness the figments of his imagination, as he had done towards the end of 'Les Poètes de sept ans':

> Avivant un agréable goût d'encre de Chine, une poudre noire pleut doucement sur ma veillée.[23] Je baisse les feux du lustre, je me jette sur le lit, et, tourné du côté de l'ombre, je vous vois, mes filles! mes reines!

It is the same powerful imagination that enables him, in another passage, to conjure up, in a few brief strokes, a picture of a sorceress appearing against the white background of a misty pond at sunset and of purple fronds swirling down:

> Le haut étang fume continuellement. Quelle sorcière va se dresser sur le couchant blanc? Quelles violettes frondaisons vont descendre?

Similarly, in the last of the passages of 'Phrases' Rimbaud imagines that he can actually hear the ringing of the bell-shaped shower of sparks released by one of the fireworks set off to celebrate some public holiday,[24] just as he had imagined, in 'Ma Bohème', that 'mes étoiles au ciel avaient un doux frou-frou':

> Pendant que les fonds publics s'écoulent en fêtes de fraternité, il sonne une cloche de feu rose dans les nuages.

This power to create a fantasy world forms the theme of the first paragraph of 'Nocturne vulgaire' in which the walls, windows and roofs within which Rimbaud is enclosed are blown away:

> Un souffle ouvre des brèches opéradiques dans les cloisons,— brouille le pivotement des toits rongés,—disperse les limites des foyers,—éclipse les croisées . . .

The process of 'reality opening out', as N. Osmond aptly describes it,[25] is continued in fairly straightforward fashion in the second paragraph with its picture of Rimbaud scrambling down a vine-covered wall, getting into a coach and driving away. But from then on the passage seems to move into a confused dream sequence

already suggested by the use of the words 'corbillard de mon sommeil' to describe the coach:

> Ici va-t-on siffler pour l'orage, et les Sodomes—et les Solymes,—
> et les bêtes féroces et les armées,
> —(Postillons et bêtes de songe reprendront-ils sous les plus
> suffocantes futaies, pour m'enfoncer jusqu'aux yeux dans la source
> de soie)
> —Et nous envoyer, fouettés à travers les eaux clapotantes et les
> boissons répandues, rouler sur l'aboi des dogues . . .

The plea for a storm to break and for 'les bêtes féroces et les
armées' to appear is reminiscent of the 'orage', the 'mille loups'
and the 'cent hordes' of 'Michel et Christine' in the poems of 1872
and these images presumably retain the same significance as symbols of the destruction of the world of modern civilization. The
allusion to 'Sodome' is no doubt linked to the relationship with
Verlaine and to the latter's 'Sonnet boiteux', written in late 1873,
in which London is described as 'cette ville de la Bible'. 'Solyme'
is the old name for Jerusalem and its presence here alongside that
of Sodom could well indicate that Rimbaud was seeking his new
Jerusalem through the medium of 'le nouvel amour'. It is difficult
to suggest such precise connotations for the remainder of the
quotation but it is to be noted that the paradoxical association of
pain and pleasure that has already been shown to be a characteristic of Rimbaud's poetry is present here in the image of people
being pushed down into silken springs and forcibly driven through
gently lapping waters. 'Nocturne vulgaire' may therefore, like
'Phrases', combine the two fundamental themes of the *Illuminations*,
the desire to escape from the confines of conventional morality and
the desire to escape from the confines of reality. If this is the case
the final line of the passage: 'Un souffle disperse les limites du
foyer', could have a double sense in that it could refer both to the
opening out of the walls of reality and also to the extension of the
accepted limits of the 'foyer conjugal'. It is worth remembering,
in this connection, that Rimbaud uses the associated word
'ménage' with reference to his relationship with Verlaine in the
1872 poem 'Jeune ménage' and in *Une Saison en enfer* where the
section 'Délires I' ends with the words 'drôle de ménage'.

But although 'Phrases' and 'Nocturne vulgaire' may therefore
combine the two themes of a new morality and a new reality,
there are many other passages in the *Illuminations* that are concerned solely with the second of these themes and that afford

Rimbaud the opportunity to transform the world around him as radically and as powerfully as he had done in, for example, 'Le Bateau ivre'. This is in fact the programme which he appears to set out for himself in the fourth section of 'Jeunesse' where, refusing to be distracted by the incidents and emotions of earlier days that are implied in the title and that are described in the first three sections, he puts these temptations behind him:

> Mais tu te mettras à ce travail: toutes les possibilités harmoniques et architecturales s'émouvront autour de ton siège. Des êtres parfaits, imprévus, s'offriront à tes expériences. Dans tes environs affluera rêveusement la curiosité d'anciennes foules et de luxes oisifs. Ta mémoire et tes sens ne seront que la nourriture de ton impulsion créatrice. Quant au monde, quand tu sortiras, que sera-t-il devenu? En tout cas, rien des apparences actuelles.

Memory and the senses will not therefore be in themselves creative but will simply provide the raw material which Rimbaud's creative impulse will then mould into new forms. The passages in which he sets out to change the face of the world in this way can be broadly divided into three categories, imaginary country scenes, imaginary city scenes, and imaginary figures, of varying degrees of difficulty and obscurity.

Among the country scenes 'Enfance III' is one of the simplest and is only slightly removed from the domain of reality by Rimbaud's child-like interest in the odd and the unusual. 'Ornières' too is an almost straightforward description except that Rimbaud successfully brings out the magical quality of the vehicles that have formed the ruts in the road that furnish the title of the passage. 'Marine', however, makes a much bolder attempt to transform reality; the land is changed into the sea and the sea into the land as Rimbaud equates ploughs[26] turning up the earth with ships cutting through the waves and, in the latter part of the passage, completes this process of re-creation by transposing words from one context to the other, referring to the currents of the land and the ruts of the sea, the pillars of the forest and the trunks of the jetty.

A passage such as 'Fleurs' is still more audacious, so much so that there is room for argument both about what precisely Rimbaud's starting-point in reality is and about the end-product of his process of re-creation:

D'un gradin d'or,—parmi les cordons de soie, les gazes grises, les velours verts et les disques de cristal qui noircissent comme du bronze au soleil,—je vois la digitale s'ouvrir sur un tapis de filigranes d'argent, d'yeux et de chevelures.

Des pièces d'or jaune semées sur l'agate, des piliers d'acajou supportant un dôme d'émeraudes, des bouquets de satin blanc et de fines verges de rubis entourent la rose d'eau.

Tels qu'un dieu aux énormes yeux bleus et aux formes de neige, la mer et le ciel attirent aux terrasses de marbre la foule des jeunes et fortes roses.

Suzanne Bernard suggests that Rimbaud's basis in reality is a theatre – hence the 'gradin d'or', the 'cordons de soie', the 'gazes grises', the 'velours verts' and the 'tapis d'yeux et de chevelures' – and that these elements are then transformed into the jewel-like flowers of the rest of the passage.[27] Antoine Adam accepts that these are the two poles of Rimbaud's creative process but he reverses the movement and sees a country scene as the basis in reality which is then transformed into a theatre.[28] Certain features in the passage seem, however, to suggest that Rimbaud's equation is in fact a much more conventional one between a forest glade and the nave of a church. The second paragraph in particular has a decidedly ecclesiastical tone with the trunks of the trees and the canopy of leaves overhead becoming 'des piliers d'acajou support-ant un dôme d'émeraudes'. The mysterious 'rose d'eau', which Suzanne Bernard finds it difficult to explain, fits readily into this context as a round pool of water metamorphosed into a rose window. The third paragraph too lacks any theatrical element but clearly endeavours to transform the sea and the sky into a statue of a god drawing towards him his crowds of wor-shippers.

Finally a passage such as 'Mystique' – as in fact the title may well be intended to imply – leaves the reader and the critic in a state of utter bewilderment as to what it is that Rimbaud has transmuted into a passage of an extraordinarily dynamic brilliance and intensity:

Sur la pente du talus les anges tournent leurs robes de laine dans les herbages d'acier et d'émeraude.

Des prés de flammes bondissent jusqu'au sommet du mamelon. A gauche le terreau de l'arête est piétiné par tous les homicides et toutes les batailles, et tous les bruits désastreux filent leur courbe. Derrière l'arête de droite la ligne des orients, des progrès.

Et tandis que la bande en haut du tableau est formée de la rumeur
tournante et bondissante des conques des mers et des nuits humaines,
   La douceur fleurie des étoiles et du ciel et du reste descend en face
du talus, comme un panier,—contre notre face, et fait l'abîme
fleurant et bleu là-dessous.

Does the use of the word 'tableau', in the third paragraph, imply
that it is an actual painting that Rimbaud is transposing into
poetry? More specifically is it the celebrated *Agneau Mystique*
hanging in the cathedral of St Bavon in Ghent which Verlaine and
Rimbaud may have visited in the summer of 1872? Or is Rimbaud simply painting his own picture of a landscape? If so does the
'talus', which is mentioned in the first and last paragraphs and
round which the whole passage seems to be focused, refer to a railway embankment? These and other suggestions have been made
by various critics who have tried in vain to identify the original
elements from which Rimbaud has created his strange world,
although the latter can, of course, and indeed should be appreciated in its own right.

Like his country scenes, Rimbaud's city scenes are sometimes
fairly straightforward descriptions and on other occasions are so
far removed from reality that it is difficult, if not impossible, to
follow their flights of fancy.

'Ville' is a good example of the first category, so much so that
almost all the critics are in agreement that Rimbaud is using London as his model and departing very little from the original. He
even adopts the standard pose of the foreigner disdainful of
English lack of taste, lack of any show of religious faith, lack of
morals, lack of elegance of speech and excessive reserve and
uniformity. 'Enfance V' also maintains its links with reality, at
least if one assumes that, in the opening line, the word 'tombeau'
is to be understood metaphorically (as indeed the verb 'louer'
suggests) and that it is the words 'mon salon souterrain' in the
third paragraph that are to be taken literally as referring to one of
the basement rooms of the houses in Howland Street, Great College Street and Stamford Street where Rimbaud lived during the
time he spent in London.[29] But from that point onwards, after an
initial opening phrase that is still founded in reality, Rimbaud's
vivid imagination takes over completely. Having already imagined
his basement room as being 'très loin sous la terre', with the
houses and fogs of London far above him 'à une distance énorme',

he now imagines he can see through the basement walls into the centre of the earth which he pictures as a microcosm of the universe:

> Moins haut, sont des égouts. Aux côtés, rien que l'épaisseur du globe. Peut-être les gouffres d'azur, des puits de feu. C'est peut-être sur ces plans que se rencontrent lunes et comètes, mers et fables.

The passage closes on the kind of ambiguous note that is so frequent in the passages concerned with 'le nouvel amour' as Rimbaud expresses a feeling of bitterness and yet, at the same time, in lines that are reminiscent of the end of 'Les Poètes de sept ans', takes pride in his ability to create his own world amidst the silence around him so that he has no need to wait for daylight to break through the basement window:

> Aux heures d'amertume je m'imagine des boules de saphir, de métal. Je suis maître du silence. Pourquoi une apparence de soupirail blêmirait-elle au coin de la voûte?

With the first of the two passages in the *Illuminations* entitled 'Villes' Rimbaud moves outside this basement room for a second description of a town, or perhaps, as the plural title may be intended to suggest, an amalgam of several towns. But this passage is very different from the more or less realistic description of London in 'Ville'. Just as he had fused land and sea in 'Marine' and a forest glade and a church in 'Fleurs', so here he sees the towns in terms of mountain landscapes:

> Ce sont des villes! C'est un peuple pour qui se sont montés ces Alleghanys et ces Libans de rêve!

The analogy is then developed in a mass of fantastic detail where one can do no more than suggest what Rimbaud's various starting points in reality may be. 'Des chalets de cristal et de bois qui se meuvent sur des rails et des poulies invisibles' could well be trains or tramcars seen from above and looking like toys moved by unseen forces. It may be the many squares and circuses in London, again seen from above, with their statues and decorative lamp-posts[30] that are transmuted into 'les vieux cratères ceints de colosses et de palmiers de cuivre [qui] rugissent mélodieusement dans les feux'. The sound of church bells in narrow streets lies much more certainly at the origin of the sentence: 'La chasse des carillons crie dans les gorges'. The mysterious 'Rolands' who sound their horns 'sur les plateformes au milieu des gouffres' are no doubt coachmen given an epic stature. In an echo of the process that had formed the theme of 'Marine', here it is the sky above the roofs that is changed into the sea, with Venus playing a dual rôle both as goddess rising from the waves and as the planet rising in the sky which darkens as a thunderstorm breaks: 'Au-dessus du niveau des plus hautes crêtes, une mer troublée par la naissance éternelle de Vénus . . . s'assombrit parfois avec des éclats mortels'. She then plays a third rôle of a more sexual nature as she enters houses transformed, in these 'Alleghanys et Libans de rêve', into caves occupied by rural rather than urban figures: 'Vénus entre dans les cavernes des forgerons et des ermites'.

It must be emphasized, however, that these are no more than suggestions as to some of the elements in reality transmuted by Rimbaud into new and exhilarating forms and that there are other images in the passage for which it is even more difficult, if not impossible, to suggest a source of inspiration. What, for instance, lies behind the following sentence: 'L'écroulement des apothéoses rejoint les champs des hauteurs où les centauresses séraphiques évoluent parmi les avalanches'? In such cases one is tempted to agree with N. Osmond that 'Rimbaud is not working from a known reality to an imaginary landscape, but attempting to create a surreality in which synthetically chosen elements fuse to form a new unity, a new dimension'.[31] But in 'Villes I' as a whole, as in 'Ville' and 'Enfance V' and as in the country scenes of the *Illuminations*, Rimbaud is doing essentially what he had done in earlier poems such as 'Ma Bohème' and 'Le Bateau ivre' – taking an ordinary, everyday scene or experience and making of it something far more exotic and compelling. And just as he had protested, at the end of 'Le Bateau ivre', that the tedium of life in Charleville could no longer satisfy him after the excitement of his earlier escapades, so at the end of 'Villes I' he asks how and when he can escape again to the dream world he has just conjured up and towards which he is longing to return:

> Quels bons bras, quelle belle heure me rendront cette région d'où viennent mes sommeils et mes moindres mouvements?

In the second passage entitled 'Villes' this Rimbaldian process of the transformation of tedious reality takes the more obvious and less successful form of a succession of superlatives:

> L'acropole officielle outre les conceptions de la barbarie moderne les plus colossales. Impossible d'exprimer le jour mat produit par ce

ciel immuablement gris, l'éclat impérial des bâtisses, et la neige
éternelle du sol. On a reproduit dans un goût d'énormité singulier
toutes les merveilles classiques de l'architecture. J'assiste à des
expositions de peinture dans des locaux plus vastes qu'Hampton
Court . . .

The dome of one of the buildings is described, exaggeratedly but
none the less prosaically, as being fifteen thousand feet in diameter
and the price of drinks as varying from eight hundred to eight
thousand rupees. But although the picture that Rimbaud thus
builds up in 'Villes II' may be less varied and less attractive than
in 'Villes I', the process he follows remains basically the same as
does, in consequence, the problem of trying to identify the starting
points in reality. Antoine Adam is convinced that many of the
references apply to Stockholm and that the passage must therefore
date from after Rimbaud's visit to Sweden in 1877.[32] V. P. Underwood is equally convinced that London, either in 1872–3 or in
1874, is the city that has furnished Rimbaud with the material
with which he creates his imaginary city.[33] But the problem is as
insoluble as in 'Villes I' since it is impossible to tell whether certain references belong to reality or to fantasy.

This is equally the case with one of the most controversial of the
passages concerned with imaginary townscapes, 'Promontoire'.
There is little doubt that the opening lines refer to a real incident
when Rimbaud was on board a ship just off some unidentified
shore:

> L'aube d'or et la soirée frissonnante trouvent notre brick en large
> en face de cette villa et de ses dépendances . . .

Even here, however, in view of the smallness of scale implied by
the word 'villa', allowance must be made for the possibility that
Rimbaud's imagination may already be at work and that a modest
boat on the Meuse, or the Seine, or the Thames may have been
enlarged into a ship at sea. From that point on there is certainly
no doubt that the typically Rimbaldian process of exaggeration
takes over as the villa and its dependencies become a promontory
as large as the mainland of Greece, or the biggest of the islands of
Japan, or the huge Arabian peninsula. Other geographical names
then follow one another in rapid succession as Rimbaud embel-
lishes his original promontory with a variety of features from a
variety of countries, most of which he had never visited so that he
can only have known of the features he mentions through having

read about them or seen illustrations of them. Among the references to Carthage, Venice, Etna, Scarborough, Brooklyn, Germany, Italy, America and Asia, it is the mention of Scarborough
that has attracted particular attention, notably from V. P. Underwood who argues that it is the promontory on which Scarborough
is situated that provides the initial inspiration of the passage and
that, since Rimbaud is more likely to have visited Scarborough in
1874 than in 1873, this passage at least must date from after *Une
Saison en enfer*.[34] Underwood readily concedes, however, not only
that the date of Rimbaud's supposed visit to Scarborough is
uncertain, but that it is equally uncertain whether he ever went to
Scarborough at all. N. Osmond points out in this connection that
Scarborough appears alongside Brooklyn which Rimbaud is
known not to have visited.[35] Moreover Underwood himself
describes a guide to Scarborough published in 1872 and reproduces some of the illustrations which, along with material from
other sources illustrating Brooklyn bridge, an eruption of Etna,
the canals of Carthage and the embankments of Venice, may well
have provided Rimbaud with the elements he needed to build up
a composite picture of his fantastic promontory, just as various
books must have provided him with the material for 'Le Bateau
ivre', written at a time when he had never even seen the sea.

Similarly in the case of 'Les Ponts' one could argue that this
passage is basically a description of the many bridges crossing the
Thames but with the scene telescoped both in space and time; but
one could equally well argue, as does Underwood,[36] that, like
'Mystique', it may be a medieval painting transposed into poetry
and given an extraordinary animation by the way Rimbaud's eye
sweeps rapidly along the lines of the bridges instead of simply
seeing the latter as so many static shapes. 'Métropolitain' has the
same dynamic quality as 'Les Ponts' but this time Rimbaud
appears to have moved much further away from reality, so much
so that the vast metropolis that he creates, although it is no doubt
based on London, as most critics agree, clearly owes much to his
own prodigious imagination.[37]

To people his fantasy world Rimbaud creates, in several passages
of the *Illuminations*, fantasy figures of a bewildering variety,
some of which are clearly transmutations of himself. This is
the case in 'Enfance IV' where, in child-like fashion, as the title
suggests, he sees himself playing a series of romantic rôles, slightly

reminiscent of his rôle as 'Petit Poucet' in 'Ma Bohème' or the boat in 'Le Bateau ivre':

> Je suis le saint, en prière sur la terrasse,—comme les bêtes pacifiques paissent jusqu'à la mer de Palestine.
> Je suis le savant au fauteuil sombre. Les branches et la pluie se jettent à la croisée de la bibliothèque.
> Je suis le piéton de la grand'route par les bois nains; la rumeur des écluses couvre mes pas. Je vois longtemps la mélancolique lessive d'or du couchant . . .

This is equally the case in 'Bottom', the original title of which was 'Métamorphoses', where Rimbaud confesses that, 'la réalité étant trop épineuse pour mon grand caractère', he had sought refuge in three imaginary rôles: 'un gros oiseau gris-bleu s'essorant vers les moulures du plafond et traînant l'aile dans les ombres de la soirée'; 'un gros ours aux gencives violettes et au poil chenu de chagrin'; and finally 'un âne, claironnant et brandissant mon grief'. (It is, of course, the third of these metamorphoses which explains the title 'Bottom', referring to the weaver in *A Midsummer Night's Dream* who is given an ass's head.) But the identity of the 'Madame' who also figures in the passage remains a mystery whose solution, as always, depends on the extent to which Rimbaud has moved away from reality in describing her. Verlaine is an obvious candidate for the rôle, especially in view of the remark of the 'vierge folle' in 'Délires I' in *Une Saison en enfer*: 'A côté de son cher corps endormi, que d'heures des nuits j'ai veillé, cherchant pourquoi il voulait tant s'évader de la réalité', and in view of Rimbaud's own comment in 'Adieu', the last chapter of *Une Saison en enfer*: 'Moi, moi qui me suis dit mage ou ange, dispensé de toute morale, je suis rendu au sol avec un devoir à chercher et la réalité rugueuse à étreindre'. It must, however, be admitted that, if 'Bottom' is similarly concerned with Rimbaud's reluctance to face up to reality at the time of his relationship with Verlaine, the second paragraph paints a picture of the latter's 'bijoux adorés' and 'chefs-d'œuvre physiques' that belong very much to the domain of fantasy. If, on the other hand, these lines are assumed to be close to reality, they clearly must refer to some unidentified woman. But in either case the theme of the passage is generally agreed to be an unsuccessful sexual relationship from which, in the final paragraph, Rimbaud escapes into the arms of prostitutes elevated to the rank of heroines of classical antiquity:

Au matin,—aube de juin batailleuse,—je courus aux champs,
âne, claironnant et brandissant mon grief, jusqu'à ce que les Sabines
de la banlieue vinrent se jeter à mon poitrail.

An equally intimate experience, but of a very different kind,
forms the theme of one of the deservedly best known and probably
most accessible of the *Illuminations*, 'Aube'. The metamorphosis
here takes the form of the personification of dawn as a goddess
whom Rimbaud pursues through the countryside and with whom
he is finally united in a moment of ecstasy not unlike that of
'Conte' or 'Veillées I', although there is no reason to think that
Verlaine or anyone else is involved in 'Aube' which is generally
agreed to be simply a moving expression of Rimbaud's love for
what he described, in a letter to Delahaye from Paris in June 1872,
as 'cette heure indicible, première du matin', adding: 'Le premier
matin en été . . . voilà ce qui m'a ravi toujours ici'.[38]

If 'Aube' is one of the most accessible of those *Illuminations* in
which Rimbaud peoples his imaginary world with imaginary
figures, 'Antique' is one of the most inaccessible passages of this
kind. In 'Aube' the identity of the goddess is made quite clear, but
in 'Antique' there is no indication of the identity or of the significance of the 'gracieux fils de Pan' who becomes an increasingly
fantastic figure in the course of the passage. Most critics have
adopted Delahaye's suggestion that Rimbaud's starting point is an
antique statue of a faun or a satyr but it is perhaps more important
to bear in mind the regret that Rimbaud had expressed in 'Soleil
et chair' at the disappearance of the days when Pan and his
followers ruled the world:

> Je regrette les temps de l'antique jeunesse,
> Des satyres lascifs, des faunes animaux . . .
> Je regrette les temps où la sève du monde,
> L'eau du fleuve, le sang rose des arbres verts
> Dans les veines de Pan mettaient un univers!

It may well be therefore that, particularly in view of a reference to
his 'double sexe', the 'fils de Pan' in 'Antique' is the symbol of
'l'amour universel' and is related to the 'Génie' of 'Conte' of
whom, as mentioned above, Rimbaud notes that 'de sa physio-
nomie et de son maintien ressortait la promesse d'un amour
multiple et complexe'.

'Being Beauteous' is similar to 'Antique' in that again the start-
point appears to be a statue of some kind, which then becomes

increasingly charged with movement and colour as the passage progresses until, in the end, having created this hallucinatory vision of a 'corps adoré' Rimbaud himself becomes one of her worshippers. But the passage ends, like so many others in the *Illuminations*, on a contrasting note as Rimbaud acknowledges the less attractive aspects of the 'beauteous being' he has created and the ordeal he feels he must undergo to persist in the creative process:

> O la face cendrée, l'écusson de crin, les bras de cristal! Le canon sur lequel je dois m'abattre à travers la mêlée des arbres et de l'air léger![39]

The first paragraph of 'Enfance I' may also have as its starting point in reality a statue of some kind, or perhaps, in view of the title, even a doll, from which Rimbaud's vivid imagination then radiates outwards to provide her with a setting as varied as it is exotic. The second paragraph describes a quite different but equally colourful figure, initially inspired perhaps by some painting or illustration that Rimbaud may have seen, unless it is simply the edge of the forest, mentioned in the opening phrase, that is the realistic background against which Rimbaud has placed his imaginary woman in an imaginary setting. The third paragraph too may be based on a painting, not however of a single woman but of a group of women all endowed by Rimbaud with the same element of mystery and fascination as the idol and girl of the first two paragraphs. Then, in a detached final line, the strangely captivating nature of these figures, which are largely, or perhaps entirely, the product of Rimbaud's imagination, is contrasted with the tedious reality of life in the company of someone who, in all probability, is to be identified as Verlaine:

> Quel ennui, l'heure du 'cher corps' et 'cher cœur'.[40]

Like the third paragraph of 'Enfance I', 'Parade' depicts a group of figures, but on this occasion, as the military and processional connotations of the title suggest, Rimbaud is presumably letting his imagination be triggered off by the soldiers who so impressed Verlaine when he and Rimbaud first came to London.[41] The military imagery then gives way to a vocabulary more characteristic of the theatre. This, in its turn is replaced by a fancy dress atmosphere with a hint of a fair-ground setting then taking over as the passage builds up to a typically Rimbaldian climax of hallucination. Finally comes the equally typical return to reality as Rimbaud emerges from his dream world and confesses to the reader:

> J'ai seul la clef de cette parade sauvage.

He might well have made a similar confession with regard to a number of other passages in the *Illuminations*. Despite the most exhaustive researches nobody has yet succeeded, for example, in providing a satisfactory key for the parade of figures named in 'Dévotion' – Louise Vanaen de Voringhem, Léonie Aubois d'Ashby, Lulu and Circeto.[42] In 'Enfance II' there is no doubt that 'les vieux qu'on a enterrés tout droits dans le rempart aux giroflées' belong to the realm of fantasy, but are 'la petite morte, derrière les rosiers' and 'le petit frère (il est aux Indes)' also figments of Rimbaud's imagination, or is he referring, as Antoine Adam believes, to the death of his younger sister Vitalie in December 1875 and to his own visit to the East Indies in the summer of 1876?[43] 'Fairy' describes offerings made to a goddess-like figure called Hélène whose identity remains a mystery and the passage laconically entitled 'H' describes an equally mysterious 'Hortense' who has been interpreted by a wide variety of critics as the symbol of a wide variety of activities in response to the final words of the passage: 'Trouvez Hortense'. In the case of such passages it seems clear that Rimbaud has moved so far into the recesses of his own private world that these figures must remain as unidentified and as unidentifiable as the more mysterious of the country scenes and the city scenes that he has created.

Disillusion

Many of the passages that have been discussed, both under the heading of 'le nouvel amour' and of 're-creation', have begun on a note of optimism but have ended on a note of disappointment as if Rimbaud has not been wholly successful in his search either for a new morality or for a new reality. There are other passages, however, which are entirely filled with a sense of disillusion and disenchantment and which must have been written at moments of profound pessimism.

'Angoisse', as the title suggests, is one such passage, where Rimbaud wonders whether, after 'les ambitions continuellement écrasées', 'les âges d'indigence' and 'notre inhabileté fatale', he can ever look forward to 'une fin aisée' and 'un jour de succès'. He doubts whether the 'franchise première' of which he had dreamed will ever be achieved. His earlier hopes of leading a crusade to a promised land and of abolishing the distinction between good and evil are powerfully, if elliptically, conveyed in a paragraph appropriately placed in parenthesis:

> (O palmes! diamant!—Amour, force!—plus haut que toutes joies et gloires!—de toutes façons, partout,—démon, dieu,— Jeunesse de cet être-ci: moi!)[44]

His present despondency is equally powerfully and equally elliptically conveyed in a final paragraph full of images of pain and silent suffering:

> Rouler aux blessures, par l'air lassant et la mer; aux supplices, par le silence des eaux et de l'air meurtriers; aux tortures qui rient, dans leur silence atrocement houleux.

'Barbare' may well be another passage of the same kind if the echoes of 'Matinée d'ivresse' in the third paragraph are taken to imply that the heady optimism of the earlier passage has now gone, save for the occasional flickers of hope, and that the old ideas of destroying the world so as to rebuild it afresh are now over:

> Remis des vieilles fanfares d'héroisme—qui nous attaquent encore le cœur et la tête—loin des anciens assassins.

In later paragraphs imagery not unlike that of 'Angoisse', but even more powerful, may be intended to convey Rimbaud's extreme anguish, interrupted by references to 'douceur', 'monde' and 'musique' as if he were looking for peace and rest:

> Douceurs!
> Les brasiers, pleuvant aux rafales de givre,—Douceurs!—les feux à la pluie du vent de diamants jetée par le cœur terrestre éternellement carbonisé pour nous.—O monde!—
> (Loin des vieilles retraites et des vieilles flammes, qu'on entend, qu'on sent,)
> Les brasiers et les écumes. La musique, virement des gouffres et choc des glaçons aux astres.
> O Douceurs, ô monde, ô musique! Et là, les formes, les sueurs, les chevelures et les yeux, flottant. Et les larmes blanches, bouillantes, —ô douceurs!—et la voix féminine arrivée au fond des volcans et des grottes arctiques . . .

The enigmatic second paragraph:

> Le pavillon en viande saignante sur la soie des mers et des fleurs
> arctiques; (elles n'existent pas),

with its conflicting connotations of suffering ('saignante') and gentleness ('soie', 'mers', 'fleurs') and of a land of peace which does not perhaps exist, may be meant to suggest the difficulties Rimbaud faced in striving to reach a goal which he feared might be illusory. The fact that these lines are repeated as the fourth paragraph and that a second repetition is begun at the very end of the passage: 'Le pavillon . . .', may indicate that the struggle is a continuing one. If this interpretation is correct, the title 'Barbare' may be related to the barbarian hordes sweeping across 'l'Europe ancienne' in 'Michel et Christine' and may confirm that the passage is concerned with Rimbaud's former desire to destroy civilization so as to restore 'la franchise première'. But it must be emphasized that this reading can only be a tentative one since 'Barbare' is among the most hermetic of the *Illuminations* and has given rise to widely divergent interpretations. N. Osmond, for example, sees it not in a pessimistic but in an optimistic sense as 'a visionary experience . . . in which contrary extremes of sensation are reconciled', [45] whereas Antoine Adam, scornful of all 'commentateurs épris de transcendence', whether of a pessimistic or an optimistic bent, sees it simply as a vivid description of the geysers and volcanoes of Iceland erupting beneath the Danish or Norwegian flag.[46]

There are no such widely divergent interpretations of 'Vagabonds' which is a disenchanted analysis of the failure of the relationship with Verlaine who is described in the opening words as a 'pitoyable frère' and whose anxiety and distress have simply exasperated his totally unsympathetic 'compagnon d'enfer':

> Et presque chaque nuit, aussitôt endormi, le pauvre frère se levait,
> la bouche pourrie, les yeux arrachés,—tel qu'il se rêvait!—et me
> tirait dans la salle en hurlant son songe de chagrin idiot.

Verlaine's view of the same situation is to be found in his sonnet 'Vers pour être calomnié' in *Jadis et naguère*:

> Ce soir je m'étais penché sur ton sommeil.
> Tout ton corps dormait chaste sur l'humble lit,
> Et j'ai vu, comme un qui s'applique et qui lit,

> Ah! j'ai vu que tout est vain sous le soleil . . .
> Vite, éveille-toi. Dis, l'âme est immortelle?

In *Une Saison en enfer* too, the 'vierge folle' expresses Verlaine's disquiet as well as his total dependence on his stronger companion:

> . . . A côté de son cher corps endormi, que d'heures des nuits j'ai veillé, cherchant pourquoi il voulait tant s'évader de la réalité . . . Je me pressentais, lui parti, en proie au vertige, précipitée dans l'ombre la plus affreuse: la mort. Je lui faisais promettre qu'il ne me lâcherait pas . . .

Rimbaud's frustration at Verlaine's inability to understand and appreciate his aims and ambitions had clearly reached breaking point at the time to which 'Vagabonds' refers and the final paragraph indicates that, although the relationship continued, it had lost its original purpose that had been so enthusiastically defined in 'Matinée d'ivresse':

> J'avais, en effet, en toute sincérité d'esprit, pris l'engagement de le rendre à son état primitif de fils du Soleil,—et nous errions, nourris du vin des cavernes et du biscuit de la route, moi pressé de trouver le lieu et la formule.

The change of pronoun from 'nous errions' to 'moi, pressé de trouver le lieu et la formule', is significant in that it indicates that Rimbaud alone was, at that stage, seeking ways and means of returning to 'la franchise première'.

But although there is general agreement among the critics as to the sense of 'Vagabonds', there is disagreement as to when it was written. It clearly describes a late stage in the relationship between Verlaine and Rimbaud, but it describes it not in the present tense, like 'Ouvriers', 'Angoisse' and 'Barbare', but in the past tense, with a past definite tense being used in the opening line:

> Pitoyable frère! Que d'atroces veillées je lui dus.

H. de Bouillane de Lacoste considers that this use of the past definite tense implies that the events related belong to the distant past and that the passage must therefore have been written in 1874.[47] But this is not the only connotation of the past definite tense; it can be used deliberately to emphasize that some recent occurrence is now definitely ended. Rimbaud could well have used it for this purpose in April or May 1873 when he had broken with Verlaine and had begun *Une Saison en enfer*, not then realizing

that the relationship was to be patched up again for a few brief
weeks from the end of May until the final quarrel in Brussels in
July 1873.

In 'Vies', as in 'Vagabonds', Rimbaud also looks back, but this
time over various aspects of his life, as the plural title implies and
as the division of the passage into three sections indicates. The first
section begins with a number of exotic references which Antoine
Adam readily takes in a literal sense as proof that it was written
after Rimbaud's return from the East Indies,[48] but which other
critics take in a metaphorical sense as evocative of Rimbaud's
former vision of a new world from which he is now exiled.[49] In the
second section, echoing the references to 'la musique savante' in
'Conte' and to 'la nouvelle harmonie' and 'le nouvel amour' in 'A
une Raison', Rimbaud describes himself in the following terms:

> Je suis un inventeur bien autrement méritant que tous ceux qui
> m'ont précédé; un musicien même qui ai trouvé quelque chose
> comme la clef de l'amour.

But he again emphasizes that he is now exiled in a country which
is usually thought to represent the Ardennes, but which may perhaps be Belgium or England, where he remembers the various
episodes in his life – his childhood, his years as an apprentice poet,
his arrival as a country boy in Paris, his quarrels, his separations
from Verlaine and his drinking bouts with his fellow poets. But
although he does not regret his past, he is sceptical both about his
achievement and about being able to make use of his new found
scepticism. These new problems by which he is troubled and the
wild anger he feels to be imminent ('j'attends de devenir un très
méchant fou') are reminiscent of the sadistic streak that has
always been perceptible in Rimbaud's work and that is to be
echoed in the claim made by the 'époux infernal' in *Une Saison en
enfer*: 'Je veux devenir bien fou de rage'. In the third section of
'Vies' Rimbaud repeats his review of his career, although emphasizing slightly different points and resorting to the familiar
exaggeration with what is perhaps an ironic comment on the
classical erudition of the Parnassian poets who gathered in
Lemerre's bookshop in the Passage Choiseul in Paris to which
Rimbaud had referred in a letter to Demeny dated 17 April 1871:

> Dans un grenier où je fus enfermé à douze ans j'ai connu le monde,
> j'ai illustré la comédie humaine. Dans un cellier j'ai appris l'histoire.
> A quelque fête de nuit dans une cité du Nord j'ai rencontré toutes

les femmes des anciens peintres. Dans un vieux passage à Paris on
m'a enseigné les sciences classiques . . .

The final lines continue the exaggerated tone before ending on a
note of extreme pessimism as if life were definitely over:

> . . . Dans une magnifique demeure cernée par l'Orient entier j'ai
> accompli mon immense œuvre et passé mon illustre retraite. J'ai
> brassé mon sang. Mon devoir m'est remis. Il ne faut même plus
> songer à cela. Je suis réellement d'outre-tombe et pas de commis-
> sions.

The difficulty with 'Vies', as with 'Vagabonds', is to decide
when this jaundiced view of past events was written. It has already
been suggested that 'Vagabonds' may date from late April or early
May 1873 and there is no reason why 'Vies' too should not have
been written at the same time. It has also been suggested that
'Solde' may have been written at a moment of renewed optimism
when Rimbaud rejoined Verlaine towards the end of May 1873
and it is interesting to compare the final line of 'Vies':

> Je suis réellement d'outre-tombe et pas de commissions,

with the final line of 'Solde' which could be, as N. Osmond
suggests,[50] a triumphant re-assessment of the situation:

> Les voyageurs n'ont pas à rendre leur commission de si tôt!

But it is equally possible that the order of the two passages should
be reversed and the final line of 'Vies' should read as a definitive
condemnation, written just before the quarrel in July 1873, of the
short-lived optimism of 'Solde'.

Such problems epitomize the extreme difficulty and indeed the
ultimate impossibility of ever arriving at an agreed solution as to
the dates when the various passages of the *Illuminations* were
written. Consequently their meaning, as has already been
emphasized on more than one occasion, must often remain a
matter for conjecture. The preceding pages have done no more
than offer an overall interpretation whose coherence may perhaps
prove persuasive, at least to those who are reluctant to believe
that the *Illuminations* are simply a collection of individual passages,
unrelated either to one another or to Rimbaud's life and work as a
whole.

The poetry of prose

Rimbaud's movement away from rigid patterns of rhyme and rhythm in the poetry of late 1871 and 1872 is continued in the *Illuminations*. The vast majority of these forty-two passages are in fact in prose, but there are nevertheless a few of them which can claim to be in verse and which still make use of the conventional techniques that Rimbaud had not entirely abandoned in the poems of 1872.

The first of the three passages under the title 'Veillées' quoted earlier, is an obvious example of a text of this kind since it is set out not as a continuous piece of prose but as six separate lines which are rhymed so as to make up a quatrain followed by a couplet. It is true that the rhymes in the quatrain are 'rimes fausses', of the kind that Rimbaud had used in the final stanza of 'La Rivière de cassis' and that in both the quatrain and the final couplet the rhymes are weak in the extreme, so that the term assonance rather than rhyme might be preferable, but nevertheless 'Veillées I' must surely rank as verse rather than prose. It is of course free verse, like 'Bonne Pensée du matin' since it has no consistent and regular rhythmic pattern, but within this broadly free structure Rimbaud has given it a rhythm of a fluid kind by creating a series of balanced elements. There is, for example, the repetition of certain verbal patterns: 'C'est le repos . . . C'est l'ami . . . C'est l'aimée . . .', at the beginning of the first three lines, followed in each case by a 'neither . . . nor' formula: 'Ni fièvre, ni langueur . . . ni ardent ni faible . . . ni tourmentante ni tourmentée . . .'. At the end of the first line the phrase 'sur le pré' echoes the one which has just preceded it, 'sur le lit', and at the end of the second and third lines 'l'ami' and 'l'aimée', which have occurred earlier in the lines, are repeated, while at the end of the fourth line this pattern of two final syllables standing in isolation is continued in 'la vie', with the whole poem being rounded off by the two balanced lines, each of six syllables, that make up the final rhyming couplet.

'Départ' is also set out in separate lines of irregular length, but although it differs from 'Veillées I' and from any of the poems of 1872 in that it is in blank verse as well as free verse, there is in fact a kind of vestigial rhyme or assonance between the first three lines, although these rhyming elements are shifted from the end to the beginning of the lines. A rhythmic quality too is conveyed by the repetition and linking together in the third line of the words 'vision' and 'rumeurs' already used in the first and second lines respectively and by the decasyllabic rhythm of the final line, divided into two groups of six and four syllables in the pattern Valéry was to adopt in 'Le Cimetière marin'.

Yet another passage set out in separate lines is 'Marine' in which, for the first time in Rimbaud's poetry, there is not the slightest trace of any regular pattern of either rhyme or rhythm. But as in 'Veillées I' and 'Départ' a flexible kind of rhythm can be detected. The first two lines have the same number of syllables and the same grammatical structure:

> Les chars d'argent et de cuivre—
> Les proues d'acier et d'argent—

This double subject is then followed by two verbs and their accompanying objects:

> Battent l'écume,—
> Soulèvent les souches des ronces.

The second part of the poem adopts the same formula of a double subject followed by a verb and its complement:

> Les courants de la lande,
> Et les ornières immenses du reflux,
> Filent circulairement vers l'est . . .

But instead of repeating exactly the structure of the first four lines by adding a second verb and its complement, Rimbaud adds two additional complements to the verb 'filer' similar to the first one, thus creating a kind of refrain:

> Vers les piliers de la forêt,—
> Vers les fûts de la jetée . . .

He then ends the poem with a long-drawn-out line that seems to absorb the shorter rhythms of the preceding lines:

> Dont l'angle est heurté par des tourbillons de lumière.

'Mouvement' too is lacking in both rhyme and in any regular rhythmic pattern, but it differs from 'Veillées I', 'Départ' and 'Marine' in that although it is set out as verse, it also lacks the more flexible rhythms that have been noted in those three poems. There is no question here of the first two lines having the same number of syllables and the same grammatical structure. Nor is there any repetition of certain words to form a kind of refrain. Nor is there the slightest trace of any rhyming elements anywhere in the lines which simply follow one another in a prosaic manner:

> Le mouvement de lacet sur la berge des chutes du fleuve,
> Le gouffre à l'étambot,
> La célérité de la rampe,
> L'énorme passade du courant
> Mènent par les lumières inouïes
> Et la nouveauté chimique
> Les voyageurs entourés des trombes du val
> Et du strom.

These four passages, 'Veillées I', 'Départ', 'Marine' and 'Mouvement' are the only ones where there are obvious and substantial traces of traditional techniques of versification,[51] but there are others in which Rimbaud has not entirely abandoned verse for prose. Several passages are set out, if not in actual lines like the four that have been discussed, at least in verses in the Biblical sense of the term, that is to say in isolated sentences or short paragraphs rather than in continuous prose. 'Après le déluge' is an example of this technique, as are the third and fourth sections of 'Enfance', 'A une Raison', the third section of 'Veillées', 'Barbare', 'Solde' and a large part of 'Génie'. In these and other passages Rimbaud also makes use of his technique of repeating the same formula to achieve a rhythmic effect. In the third section of 'Enfance', for example, every line, or rather every verse, begins with 'Il y a . . .' and in the fourth section there is the same kind of refrain effect: 'Je suis le saint . . . Je suis le savant . . . Je suis le piéton . . .'. In 'A une Raison' there is a similar use of repetition, or near repetition which succeeds in transforming the paragraphs into verses:

> Un coup de ton doigt sur le tambour décharge tous les sons et commence la nouvelle harmonie.
> Un pas de toi c'est la levée des nouveaux hommes et leur en-marche.
> Ta tête se détourne: le nouvel amour! Ta tête se retourne,—le nouvel amour! . . .

Six out of the eight paragraphs of 'Solde' begin with the cry: 'A vendre' and every paragraph of 'Dévotion' begins with the same dedicatory formula: 'A ma sœur Louise Vanaen de Voringhem . . .

A ma sœur Léonie Aubois d'Ashby . . . A Lulu,—démon . . . A l'adolescent que je fus . . .', while every paragraph of 'Métropolitain' ends with a noun standing in apposition to the rest of the paragraph and apparently summing up its contents: '. . .—la ville . . . —la bataille . . . —la campagne . . . —le ciel . . . —ta force'. In 'Barbare' not only is the word 'douceurs' repeated four times in different places, linked, on the last occasion, with two other words that have occurred before: 'O Douceurs, ô monde, ô musique!' but there is also a more regular refrain in that, as has been mentioned above, the second verse

> Le pavillon en viande saignante sur la soie des mers et des fleurs arctiques; (elles n'existent pas.),

s repeated as the fourth verse and is started once more at the very end of the passage as if the refrain were to be repeated for the third time: 'Le pavillon . . .'. Finally, in 'Génie' there are several examples, and subtly varied examples, of this technique of repetition. The opening phrase of the passage: 'Il est l'affection et le présent . . .', is picked up and modified at the beginning of the next sentence: 'Il est l'affection et l'avenir, la force et l'amour . . .', which leads on to a different echo at the beginning of the next paragraph: 'Il est l'amour...'. Towards the end of this same passage the exclamatory phrases which open each paragraph not only echo one another in their structure: 'O ses souffles . . . Son corps! . . . Sa vue, sa vue! . . . Son jour! . . .' but these words are then grouped together in the very last line of the text: 'Suivre ses vues, ses souffles, son corps, son jour'. And in the final paragraph leading into this last line Rimbaud achieves a balanced rhythmic phrasing by using a succession of 'de ceci à cela' constructions:

> Sachons, cette nuit d'hiver, de cap en cap, du pôle tumultueux au château, de la foule à la plage, de regards en regards . . .

It is worth noting too that the opening line of the final paragraph of 'Génie' has the rhythm of a classically balanced alexandrine:

> Il nous a connus tous, et nous a tous aimés,

as has the penultimate sentence of 'Antique':

> Ton cœur bat dans ce ventre où dort le double sexe.

There are occasionally other examples too in the *Illuminations* of key lines whose rhythm is that of a twelve syllable line of poetry, such as the last line of 'A une Raison':

> Arrivée de toujours, qui t'en iras partout,

the last line of 'Parade':

> J'ai seul la clef de cette parade sauvage,

and the final phrase of 'Ornières' which is reminiscent of a Romantic 'trimètre' rather than a classical 'tétramètre':

> . . . filant au trot des grandes juments bleues et noires,

The fifth section of 'Phrases' begins with a 'tétramètre' and ends with a 'trimètre' and indeed, short though the text is, it deserves almost to rank as verse rather than prose, thanks to these opening and closing alexandrines and to the regular rhythm imparted by the repetition, as in 'Veillées I', 'Marine' and the last paragraph of 'Génie', of the same grammatical pattern:

> J'ai tendu des cordes de clocher à clocher; des guirlandes de fenêtre à fenêtre; des chaînes d'or d'étoile à étoile, et je danse.

The sixth section of 'Phrases' also begins and ends with an alexandrine and again the repetition of the same grammatical pattern gives a rhythmic effect:

> Le haut étang fume continuellement. Quelle sorcière va se dresser sur le couchant blanc. Quelles violettes frondaisons vont descendre.

Not only a concealed rhythm but what one might call a concealed rhyme can also be detected in these lines, since 'continuellement' and 'couchant blanc' read like a rhyme in a piece of verse and 'frondaisons' and 'vont descendre' like one of those approximate rhymes that Rimbaud had used so frequently in his verse poems of 1872. 'Fleurs' is an equally striking example of this technique at the beginning of the final paragraph:

> Tels qu'un dieu aux énormes yeux bleus et aux formes de neige, la mer et le ciel attirent aux terrasses de marbre la foule des jeunes et fortes roses.

A modification of the same technique can be perceived both here and in the first paragraph of 'Fleurs' where Rimbaud makes an obvious use of alliteration and assonance to lift his text out of the domain of ordinary prose:

> D'un gradin d'or,—parmi les cordons de soie, les gazes grises, les
> velours verts et les disques de cristal qui noircissent comme du bronze
> au soleil, —je vois la digitale s'ouvrir sur un tapis de filigranes
> d'argent, d'yeux et de chevelures . . .

In 'Ornières' too Rimbaud is clearly making use of alliteration in
the opening phrase where the labial consonants 'f', 'v', 'b' and
'p' cluster together to give a softening effect:

> A droite l'aube d'été éveille les feuilles et les vapeurs et les bruits
> de ce coin du parc . . .

and in the following phrase the constant repetition of the vowel 'i'
adds to the effect of peace and quiet:

> . . . et les talus de gauche tiennent dans leur ombre violette les mille
> rapides ornières de la route humide . . .

But although there are a good many passages of the *Illuminations*
where such traces of conventional poetic processes can be found to
a greater or lesser degree, in the majority of passages Rimbaud has
broken away completely from these particular methods and has
resorted to other means of attaining a poetic quality, among which
the principal one is the use of imagery. This has, of course, always
had an important rôle to play in poetry, and especially in Rimbaud's poetry, where the power of such poems as 'Le Bateau ivre'
and 'Voyelles' resides largely in their profusion of vivid imagery.
But in the *Illuminations*, as Rimbaud abandons more and more the
use of rhyme and rhythm, he comes to depend more and more on
imagery to lift his passages out of the realm of prose into that of
poetry. The final paragraph of 'Génie' is a notable example of the
way in which this technique supplements the flexible rhythm that
has already been mentioned. The notion of people in distress is
translated into the image of 'cette nuit d'hiver', the universal
appeal that is launched is conveyed through a series of wide
ranging images: 'de cap en cap, du pôle tumultueux au château,
de la foule à la plage, de regards en regards' and the divine nature
of the 'génie' is given physical expression by the picture of a giant
figure striding ahead 'sous les marées et au haut des déserts de
neige'. In the fifth section of 'Phrases' too the unusual and vivid
imagery undoubtedly contributes, along with the rhythmic qualities that have been mentioned, to the poetic effect of this short
text. This is equally the case with 'Barbare' where the sub-

stitution of the adjectival phrase 'en viande saignante' for 'rouge' to describe 'le pavillon' in the refrain, is so much more compelling than a straightforward colour adjective would have been. This is immediately followed by the contrastingly cool and restful images of 'la soie des mers et des fleurs arctiques' which then develop into the extraordinarily powerful images of ice and snow on the one hand and of fire and flame on the other which make a major contribution to the arresting quality of 'Barbare'. The same is true of 'Marine' whose opening and closing lines in particular have, in addition to their rhythmic quality, a scintillating effect obtained through references to metals and to whirlpools of light. In 'Fleurs' too the brilliant visual images of the 'gradins d'or', the 'disques de cristal qui noircissent comme du bronze au soleil', the 'filigranes d'argent', the 'pièces d'or jaune semées sur l'agate', the 'dôme d'émeraudes' and the 'fines verges de rubis' join forces with the auditive effects to make of this passage one of the most captivating of the *Illuminations*, however enigmatic its meaning may be.

In passages where rhyme and rhythm has been totally abandoned a correspondingly greater burden is borne by the imagery in the creation of a poetic quality, as is the case with many of the texts describing an urban or rural landscape. 'Villes I', for example, makes use of a succession of powerful and varied images:

> Ce sont des villes! C'est un peuple pour qui se sont montés ces Alleghanys et ces Libans de rêve! Des chalets de cristal et de bois qui se meuvent sur des rails et des poulies invisibles. Les vieux cratères ceints de colosses et de palmiers de cuivre rugissent mélodieusement dans les feux . . .

The same kind of extraordinary accumulation of images gives 'Promontoire' its compelling effect:

> L'aube d'or et la soirée frissonnante trouvant notre brick en large en face de cette villa et de ses dépendances, qui forment un promontoire aussi étendu que l'Epire et le Péloponnèse, ou que la grande île du Japon, ou que l'Arabie! Des fanums qu'éclaire la rentreé des théories, d'immenses vues de la défense des côtes modernes; des dunes illustrées de chaudes fleurs et de bacchanales; de grands canaux de Carthage et des Embankments d'une Venise louche; de molles éruptions d'Etnas et des crevasses de fleurs et d'eaux des glaciers . . .

'Aube' too, though it is very different in tone, engages in the same fundamental process, counting on a swift succession of varied images:

> J'ai embrassé l'aube d'été. Rien ne bougeait encore au front des palais. L'eau était morte. Les camps d'ombre ne quittaient pas la route du bois. J'ai marché, réveillant les haleines vives et tièdes, et les pierreries regardèrent, et les ailes se levèrent sans bruit ...

Throughout the *Illuminations* Rimbaud has a particular predilection for images of fire and flame and hard reflecting surfaces. 'Barbare', 'Marine' and 'Fleurs' have already been noted in this respect, but 'Aube' too refers not only to 'pierreries' but also to 'frais et blèmes éclats', to 'la cime argentée' and to 'les quais de marbre'. Similarly 'Villes I' mentions not only 'des chalets de cristal' and 'les vieux cratères [qui] rugissent mélodieusement dans les feux', but also 'des vêtements et des oriflammes éclatants comme la lumière des cimes', 'l'ardeur du ciel', 'des perles et des conques précieuses', 'des robes opalines' and 'des châteaux bâtis en os'. Precious stones, metals and fire also play their part in the opening lines of 'Mystique':

> Sur la pente du talus les anges tournent leurs robes de laine dans les herbages d'acier et d'émeraude.
> Des prés de flammes bondissent jusqu'au sommet du mamelon ...

and in Rimbaud's transformation of his basement room in 'Enfance V' into a kind of planet whirling through space:

> Aux côtés rien que l'épaisseur du globe. Peut-être les gouffres d'azur, des puits de feu. C'est peut-être sur ces plans que se rencontrent lunes et comètes, mers et fables.
> Aux heures d'amertume je m'imagine des boules de saphir, de métal ...

Though the examples of such striking images in the *Illuminations* are legion, so that one can do no more, in the limited space available in this study, than draw attention to their fundamental importance, mention might be made of three last examples which illustrate particularly well Rimbaud's genius in this respect. One is the final paragraph of 'Royauté' where the images of purple hangings and gardens of palms are suggestive of a royal and even a divine triumph, however brief its duration may have been:[52]

> En effet, ils furent rois toute une matinée où les tentures carminées
> se relevèrent sur les maisons, et toute l'après-midi, où ils s'avancèrent
> du côté des jardins de palmes.

Another one is at the very end of the second section of 'Enfance'
where Rimbaud finds an image of compelling sadness to describe
the sea:

> Les nuées s'amassaient sur la haute mer faite d'une éternité de
> chaudes larmes.

The third and final example, from the fourth section of 'Enfance',
is no less compellingly sad, but it is the unusually homely term
used to describe the sunset which gives this phrase its striking
originality:

> Je vois longtemps la mélancolique lessive d'or du couchant.

It is therefore by the occasional use of vestigial rhymes, by the
more frequent use of fluid rhythms and by the constant use of
vivid and arresting imagery that Rimbaud achieves a poetic
quality in the *Illuminations*. But he also lifts them out of the realm
of prose by the use of an extraordinarily dynamic style where normal syntax is abandoned.[53] 'Promontoire', for example, although
it begins in a conventional way with a subject, a verb, an object
and an adverbial phrase (and it is one of the comparatively few
passages in the *Illuminations* to do this), soon develops into a series
of phrases without any verb as Rimbaud notes down a succession
of images without integrating them into a rounded sentence.
'Ornières' is a similar passage in this respect, beginning in a syn-
tactically straightforward way but then becoming a series of
quickly noted images which are not inserted into the framework of
a conventional sentence. 'Les Ponts' reverses this process, plunging
into a series of rapid notations and only slowing down into normal
syntax towards the middle of the passage. 'Parade' begins in the
same dynamic fashion and only in the second paragraph does the
passage adopt a more leisurely pace. Several of the *Illuminations*
begin in this way, with a verbless opening phrase, often couched
in the vocative, which catches the reader's attention, before
resorting to a more normal syntax: 'Gracieux fils de Pan! . . .'
('Antique'); 'Devant une neige un Etre de Beauté de haute
taille . . .' ('Being Beauteous'); 'O les énormes avenues du pays
saint . . .' ('Vies'); 'Une matinée couverte en juillet . . .' ('Phrases
IV'); 'O cette chaude matinée de février . . .' ('Ouvriers');

'Pitoyable frère . . .' ('Vagabonds'); 'Homme de constitution ordinaire . . .' ('Jeunesse II').

Other passages consist exclusively of a series of notations with not a single finite verb throughout. This is the case with the second and third paragraphs of 'Enfance I' describing the 'fille à lèvre d'orange' and the 'dames qui tournoient sur les terrasses voisines de la mer'. It can also be said to be true of the first paragraph since the one apparently finite verb in fact lies within a subordinate clause qualifying the opening noun which remains without a verb:

> Cette idole, yeux noirs et crin jaune, sans parents ni cour, plus noble que la fable, mexicaine et flamande; son domaine, azur et verdure insolents, court sur des plages nommées, par des vagues sans vaisseaux, de noms férocement grecs, slaves, celtiques.

'Dévotion' too, since it is made up of a series of dedicatory phrases, consists therefore, grammatically speaking, of a succession of indirect objects to which a subject, verb and direct object are never added.

In such cases it can reasonably be argued that Rimbaud has abandoned normal grammar and syntax deliberately, but there are other passages in the *Illuminations* which seem to have an unintentionally faulty structure and which give the impression that Rimbaud has lost the thread of what he originally intended to write. 'Barbare' is perhaps the most striking example of a passage of this kind. It begins with an adverbial phrase of time, after which one would expect a statement with a main verb, but in fact Rimbaud slips into what is in effect a parenthetical phrase, the latter part of which is qualified by a clause actually in parenthesis:

> Bien après les jours et les saisons, et les êtres et les pays,
> Le pavillon en viande saignante sur la soie des mers et des fleurs arctiques; (elles n'existent pas.)

He then uses a past participle which further gives the impression that he is so far merely setting the scene:

> Remis des vieilles fanfares d'héroïsme—qui nous attaquent encore le cœur et la tête—loin des anciens assassins—

But instead of now introducing the expected main clause he repeats the second phrase of the passage as a refrain which is then followed by the isolated exclamation: 'Douceurs!'. Then comes a succession of phrases evoking the opposite feeling to 'douceurs' with this word repeated in parenthesis to point the contrast:

> Les brasiers, pleuvant aux rafales de givre,—Douceurs!—les feux à la pluie du vent de diamants jetée par le cœur terrestre éternellement carbonisé pour nous.—O monde!—

This is followed by another phrase in parenthesis looking back to the past and echoing the end of the third phrase:

> (Loin des vieilles retraites et des vieilles flammes, qu'on entend, qu'on sent,)

Then comes a phrase which consists solely of a succession of nouns and which is clearly a variation on the earlier phrase evoking contrasting feelings of pain and gentleness:

> Les brasiers et les écumes. La musique, virement des gouffres et choc des glaçons aux astres.

The penultimate paragraph is also a succession of nouns, again evoking contrasting feelings of pain and gentleness, but with two participles inserted, one present and one past:

> O Douceurs, ô monde, ô musique! Et là, les formes, les sueurs, les chevelures et les yeux, flottant. Et les larmes blanches, bouillantes,— ô douceurs!—et la voix féminine arrivée au fond des volcans et des grottes arctiques.

The passage then comes to an end with the partial repetition of the second phrase which has already been used once as a refrain: 'Le pavillon . . .', without Rimbaud ever having reached the point of making a statement, or, in grammatical terms, of bringing in his expected main clause.

In a similar fashion he seems to have lost the thread of the final long and complex sentence in 'Ville' which begins with a subordinate clause: 'Aussi comme, de ma fenêtre, je vois des spectres nouveaux roulant à travers l'épaisse et éternelle fumée de charbon', and then, after a short phrase in parenthesis, '—notre ombre des bois, notre nuit d'été—', continues with another phrase in apposition to 'spectres nouveaux': 'des Erynnies nouvelles, devant mon cottage qui est ma patrie et tout mon cœur puisque tout ici ressemble à ceci'. This is followed by a long phrase in apposition to 'ceci': '—la Mort sans pleurs, notre active fille et servante, et un Amour désespéré, et un joli Crime piaulant dans la boue de la rue', after which one would expect the main clause of the sentence, since everything has so far been dependent on the preposition 'comme', but in fact this expected main clause fails to materialize and the sentence simply peters out.

The second paragraph of 'Fairy' should be noted in this connection too, since it is generally agreed to be incomprehensible as it stands and critics have suggested the insertion of a comma in different places and various different ways of reading the sentence to try and make reasonable sense of it: '—Après le moment de l'air des bûcheronnes à la rumeur du torrent sous la ruine des bois, de la sonnerie des bestiaux à l'écho des vals, et des cris des steppes.—'

'Mouvement' is another oddly constructed passage in which there is little doubt that two dashes are misplaced towards the end and that Rimbaud meant to write: 'On voit—roulant comme une digue au-delà de la route hydraulique motrice, monstrueux, s'éclairant sans fin,—leur stock d'études', and not, as he in fact does write: '—On voit, roulant comme un digue au-delà de la route hydraulique motrice, monstrueux, s'éclairant sans fin,—leur stock d'études'. Similarly, even allowing for the fact that Rimbaud makes use of dashes in a particularly idiosyncratic fashion, there seems no justification for the dash at the end of the second paragraph of 'Enfance V' and no reason why, in the case of two exactly parallel phrases in 'A une Raison', one should have a colon inserted and the other a comma and a dash:

> Ta tête se détourne: le nouvel amour! Ta tête se retourne,—le nouvel amour!

At the beginning of 'Vagabonds' it is not Rimbaud's use of dashes but his use of inverted commas which seems faulty in that he appears to indicate incorrectly the change from direct to indirect speech; he no doubt meant to write:

> Pitoyable frère! Que d'atroces veillées je lui dus! 'Je ne me saisissais pas fervemment de cette entreprise'. Je m'étais joué de son infirmité. Par ma faute nous retournerions en exil, en esclavage.

He in fact confuses the 'je' in quotation marks above with the 'je' in the remainder of the passage and thus attributes to the 'pitoyable frère' contradictory statements:

> Pitoyable frère! Que d'atroces veillées je lui dus! 'Je ne me saisissais pas fervemment de cette entreprise. Je m'etais joué dé son infirmité. Par ma faute nous retournerions en exil, en esclavage'.

Among other mistakes of a broadly similar kind it has been suggested that in 'Barbare' he meant to write: 'les feux à la pluie de diamants' and that he inserted the words 'du vent' inadvertently after the word 'pluie'. At the end of 'Villes II' there is a curious phrase: 'Les gentilhommes sauvages chassent leurs chroniques', and it has been suggested that there is a noun missing in front of the adjective 'chroniques'. At the beginning of 'Promontoire' Rimbaud makes so obvious a mistake in writing 'notre brick en large' that in his edition of the *Oeuvres complètes* Antoine Adam takes the liberty of correcting it to 'au large'. He does not, however, take a similar liberty with the incorrect and cacaphonous use of 'au haut' towards the end of 'Génie' where Rimbaud presumably meant to write: 'sous les marées et en haut des déserts de neige'.

As well as these errors in the construction of his sentences Rimbaud makes frequent mistakes in spelling and punctuation, carefully noted by Albert Py in his edition of the *Illuminations*. In the very first line of the very first passage, 'Après le Déluge', 'fut' is given an incorrect circumflex accent and elsewhere in the same text 'églogues' has no accent, 'Déluges' is written with a grave instead of an acute accent and the pronoun 'ils' in the final paragraph has no 's'. In the second passage, 'Enfance', the word 'prés' is wrongly given a grave accent on two occasions, two clearly necessary commas are omitted after 'pèlerinages' and 'tyranniques' in the penultimate paragraph and 'là-dedans' and 'au-dessus' are unhyphenated. 'Parade' omits an acute accent on 'bohémiens' and 'Matinée d'ivresse' gives 'créés' one accent instead of two. 'Les Ponts' leaves out the hyphen in 'quelques-uns' and 'Ville' transposes the 'y' and the 'i' as well as incorrectly doubling the 'n' in 'Erinyes'. 'Villes I' leaves out not only the hyphen but also the plural 's' on the adjectival part of the word 'plates-formes' as well as omitting the hyphen in 'au-dessus' and 'là-haut'. In 'Villes II' Rimbaud writes 'huit cent' instead of 'huit cents'. In 'Veillées II' 'atmosphériques' has a superfluous 'h' after the 't', although the same word is spelt correctly in 'Mouvement' where the word 'accidents' also occurs, for which 'accidences' in 'Veillées II' is probably a mistake. In 'Nocturne vulgaire' 'éclipse' and 'véhicule' are both written without accents. In 'Métropolitain' Rimbaud writes 'longeur' instead of 'longueur' and in 'Fairy' 'des cri' instead of 'des cris'. In 'Promontoire' 'défense' has a grave instead of an acute accent and 'éruptions' has no accent at all. Similarly in 'Scènes' 'évolue' is written without an acute accent and 'mû' without a circumflex accent.

In addition to these undoubted errors, other probable or possible mistakes can be suggested. In 'Vies I' 'la main de la campagne' is probably a slip for 'la main de la compagne'. At the end of 'Enfance V' 'mers et fables' seems likely to be a mistake for 'mers et sables'. In 'Villes I' it seems possible that 'les canaux pendus derrière les chalets' should read 'les fanaux pendus derrière les chalets'. Towards the end of 'Mouvement' 'la roue hydraulique motrice' would make sense whereas 'la route hydraulique motrice' does not. In 'Nocturne vulgaire' 'des toits rongés' makes less sense than 'des toits rangés' and in 'Mystique', when Rimbaud writes 'le terreau de l'arête est piétiné', he may well have meant to write 'le terrain de l'arête est piétiné'.

For Rimbaud to have made so many mistakes of grammar, syntax, spelling and punctuation in his manuscript calls for an explanation, all the more so because the vast majority of the passages of the *Illuminations* are written on one side of the paper only[54] and contain very few corrections.[55] This suggests that the manuscript was intended as a final version and yet the mistakes listed above are the kind that would occur in a first version before the writer had revised his text to adjust faulty or unfinished sentences and to check punctuation and spelling. The answer to this apparent paradox, that the presentation is that of a final version although the mistakes are those of a first version, could well be that the manuscript is both the one and the other.[56] In accordance with the ideas expressed in the 'lettre du voyant', Rimbaud may have let his ideas unfold without consciously intervening to control, adjust and revise them. 'J'assiste à l'éclosion de ma pensée, je la regarde, je l'écoute . . .', seems virtually a definition of the *Illuminations*, and just as Rimbaud wrote in the 'lettre du voyant', introducing one of his poems, 'j'ai l'archet en main, je commence', implying that once he had given the initial 'coup d'archet', the violin then played on of its own accord, similarly one could well imagine him saying the same thing about the cascading imagery of so many of the passages of the *Illuminations*. The even more celebrated phrase from the 'lettre du voyant': 'Le poète se fait voyant par un long, immense et raisonné dérèglement de tous les sens', suggesting that Rimbaud deliberately gave free rein to his creative gifts and rejected all notion of revision and careful composition, seems equally applicable to the visionary scenes and fantasy creatures of the *Illuminations*. If this is so it means that Rimbaud, finally breaking completely free from the last constraints of rhyme and rhythm by which he had still been bound, however loosely, in the poems of 1872, puts fully into practice in the *Illuminations* the ideas advanced in the 'lettre du voyant'.

V

UNE SAISON EN ENFER: 1873

Publication and composition

With the exception of a few of his early poems, *Une Saison en enfer* is the only one of Rimbaud's works to have been published immediately after its composition. But even so, its publication, in the autumn of 1873, was accompanied by a number of complications, not the least of which is that it is not strictly correct to say that *Une Saison en enfer* was *published*; in actual fact five hundred copies were *printed* but they were not then offered for sale to the public. Rimbaud received his half-dozen author's copies, but all the others were left in the hands of the printers, presumably because Rimbaud was unable or unwilling to pay for them. It goes without saying that the publication of work such as *Une Saison en enfer* must have been undertaken at the author's expense and Rimbaud was no doubt required, as is the usual practice, to pay part of the cost in advance and the rest on completion. It is this latter part of the agreement that he presumably failed to observe and in consequence the printers concerned, M. J. Poot & Co., 37 rue aux Choux, Brussels, took no further steps to distribute the copies to the general public. Rimbaud sent his half-dozen complimentary copies to various friends, including Verlaine and Delahaye, none of whom appear to have urged him or helped him to bring his volume to the notice of the press or the public, with the result that, as Verlaine put it ten years later in *Les Poètes maudits* in 1883: '*Une Saison en enfer* sombra corps et biens dans un oubli monstrueux'.

It was not until 1901, quite by chance, that the remainder of the five hundred copies was discovered in the storeroom of Poot & Co., but in the meantime, the picturesque legend had been launched, by Isabelle Rimbaud and her husband Paterne Berrichon, that Rimbaud had burned all the copies of *Une Saison en enfer* in 1873 in a superb gesture of renunciation, a mere half-dozen having been saved from the flames. It was not until after 1914, when the discoverer of the five hundred copies made his discovery generally known that this legend began to disappear from biographies of Rimbaud.[1]

Not only do complications thus surround the initial printing and ultimate publication of *Une Saison en enfer*, but further complications surround the circumstances of its composition. At the end of the last chapter Rimbaud adds the dates: 'Avril–août, 1873' and it is generally agreed that these dates refer, as is customary with indications of this kind, to the period of composition. N. Osmond's suggestion that these dates 'correspond to the duration of Rimbaud's season in hell, not to the actual composition of the work', is difficult to accept, not only because this is not the usual significance of a dating of this sort, but also because the period April–August 1873 does not form a single, distinctive phase in Rimbaud's life. On the contrary, it is divided into two very different parts – the six weeks from 11 April to 24 May when he was with his family at Roche,[2] and the eight weeks from 24 May to the end of July when he had rejoined Verlaine and was with him in London and Brussels during the final unhappy stage of their relationship. The duration of Rimbaud's season in hell could therefore be regarded either as these last few disastrous weeks with Verlaine from late May to late July, or as the much longer period covering the whole of the time they spent together from late 1871 to mid 1873, but there seems to be no good reason for drawing a line somewhere between the two.

On the other hand it may be thought that the five months from April to August 1873 form too long a time for the composition of a work which is a mere twenty-five pages long and gives the impression of having been written under intense emotional pressure. The solution to this problem may be that when Rimbaud parted from Verlaine after crossing the Channel with him on 4 April and arrived home at Roche on 11 April he regarded his attempt during the previous months to create a new morality and a new poetry as having failed.[3] The postscript of his letter of 18 May to Delahaye makes it clear that he had no wish to meet Verlaine again, even though the latter was a mere thirty miles away staying with relatives at Jehonville in south-east Belgium, and that he had every intention of staying in Roche or Charleville for some considerable time: 'Je rouvre ma lettre. Verlaine doit t'avoir proposé un rendez-vol au dimanche 18, à Boulion. Moi je ne puis y aller. Si tu y vas il te chargera probablement de quelques fraguemants en prose de moi ou de lui, à me retourner. La mère Rimb. retournera à Charlestown dans le courant de juin. C'est sûr, et je tâcherai de rester dans cette jolie ville quelque temps'.[4]

Moreover, it is generally agreed that he is referring to what was ultimately to become *Une Saison en enfer* when he writes, in the same letter: 'Je travaille pourtant assez régulièrement, je fais de petites histoires en prose, titre général: Livre païen, ou Livre nègre . . .' It is true that, as N. Osmond points out,[5] the term 'petites histoires' does not apply particularly well to *Une Saison en enfer* in its final form, but at this early stage Rimbaud may have intended his 'Livre païen ou Livre nègre' to have a different structure more suited to such a description. More important than the question of form is the undoubted fact that the opposition between Christianity and paganism and between white civilization and black primitivism, implicit in the earlier titles, remains one of the principal themes of *Une Saison en enfer*.

But although it therefore seems probable that Rimbaud felt, during the last two weeks in April and the first three weeks of May 1873, that his brave attempt to create a new world had ended in failure and although it seems certain that he had already begun to adopt the ideas that were to dominate *Une Saison en enfer*, he suddenly changed his mind and not only went to meet Verlaine at Bouillon on 24 May but promptly set off for London with him to resume their interrupted relationship which finally came to an end with the shooting incident and Verlaine's arrest in Brussels on 10 July. When Rimbaud once more returned to Roche towards the end of July the disillusionment and disappointment he had felt in April must have been all the stronger now that yet another effort to forge a lasting relationship with Verlaine had ended so disastrously. It could well be therefore that, under the impact of this second traumatic separation from Verlaine, he returned to the 'Livre païen ou Livre Nègre' that he had begun three months before and completed it in a different form and under the new title of *Une Saison en enfer*.

Before turning to a discussion of the sense of *Une Saison en enfer*, mention must be made of three short passages that Rimbaud also wrote about this time. These are the texts generally known as the 'proses évangéliques' based on the fourth and fifth chapters of *The Gospel according to St John*. Since they are written on one side only of two sheets of paper having on the other side rough drafts of two parts of *Une Saison en enfer* it seems certain that they must have been written before these rough drafts which would otherwise have flowed over on to the blank reverse sides, as is in fact the case with the rough draft of a third part of *Une Saison en enfer*. There is, of course, no means of knowing just how long before the rough drafts the 'proses évangéliques' were written, but it seems reasonable to suggest that it cannot have been long before. It is even possible that these three short texts may be the 'petites histoires en prose' to which Rimbaud refers in his letter of 18 May as forming part of his 'Livre païen ou Livre nègre' especially since, at the end of the letter, he states that he has already written three of them. They undoubtedly fit the description of 'petites histoires' since they describe three incidents in the life of Christ, namely his revelation of his identity to the woman of Samaria, the miracle by which he cured the son of a nobleman from Capernaum and the miracle by which he cured a cripple at the pool of Bethsaïda. Whether or not they could also be seen as forming part of a 'Livre païen' depends on how these curious and enigmatic passages are interpreted, for although they are based on the Bible thay have a strange twist to them which suggests to many critics that Rimbaud is denying that Christ possessed any miraculous gifts. Other critics, however, do not see them as anti-Christian but simply as somewhat elliptic renderings of the original Bible stories. Whatever view one takes of them their fundamental significance no doubt lies in the fact that they are concerned with the question of the power of the Christian faith. Their ambiguity may therefore be a reflection of the anxiety that Rimbaud felt on this issue in April and May 1873 and that can also be perceived in *Une Saison en enfer*.

Changed attitudes

Although *Une Saison en enfer* is divided into seven chapters preceded by a brief preface it can also be divided into three distinct parts dealing with quite different and virtually unrelated themes. The long first chapter, 'Mauvais Sang', the short second chapter 'Nuit de l'enfer', the equally short fourth chapter, 'L'Impossible', and the even shorter fifth, sixth and seventh chapters, 'L'Eclair', 'Matin' and 'Adieu', are all concerned with moral and religious issues. The third chapter, however, 'Délires', forms a parenthesis interrupting, for no apparent reason, the tumultuous flow of Rimbaud's thoughts and feelings on these issues so as to deal with two quite different matters in the two fairly lengthy sections into which it is sub-divided.

'*Drôle de ménage*'

The first of these sections, which bears the sub-heading 'Vierge folle—l'époux infernal', is generally agreed to be, as has already been suggested on a number of occasions in the course of the preceding pages, a disenchanted account of the relationship between Rimbaud and Verlaine.[6] It is written in the form of a monologue by the latter, introduced by a single opening line spoken by the former:[7] 'Ecoutons la confession d'un compagnon d'enfer', and brought to a close by a final caustic comment by Rimbaud: 'Drôle de ménage!' All the rest of the text in between these opening and closing lines is in inverted commas and is therefore the confession of the 'compagnon d'enfer', within which there are further sets of inverted commas as the 'vierge folle' quotes the ideas and opinions of 'l'époux infernal'.

By means of these somewhat complex methods 'Délires I' paints a vivid portrait of Rimbaud, emphasizing certain aspects of his character that have already been noted elsewhere in his work. His sense of living in an alien world, apparent in such texts as 'Soleil et chair' and 'Après le déluge', is repeated even more forcefully in 'Délires I':

> . . . Je suis de race lointaine: mes pères étaient Scandinaves: ils se perçaient les côtes, buvaient leur sang . . .

This claim, which is also made in other chapters of *Une Saison en enfer*, is clearly symbolical of Rimbaud's conviction that he does not by nature belong to modern, Christian civilization and it is the consequent sense of frustration and anger that drives him into a masochistic rage:

> . . . Je me ferai des entailles partout le corps, je me tatouerai, je veux devenir hideux comme un Mongol: tu verras, je hurlerai dans les rues. Je veux devenir bien fou de rage . . .

But his anger can be directed against others as well as himself and, like the prince in 'Conte', he derives a sadistic pleasure from terrifying others, as the 'vierge folle' sadly complains:

> Je l'écoute faisant de l'infamie une gloire, de la cruauté un charme . . . Les nuits, souvent, ivre, il se poste dans des rues ou dans des maisons, pour m'épouvanter mortellement.

In sharp contrast to this side of Rimbaud's character the extraordinary tenderness towards less fortunate members of society that is revealed in such early poems as 'Les Effarés' and 'Le Dormeur du val' is again emphasized by the words of the 'vierge folle':

... Dans les bouges où nous nous enivrions, il pleurait en considérant ceux qui nous entouraient, bétail de la misère. Il relevaient les ivrognes dans les rues noires. Il avait la pitié d'une mère méchante pour les petits enfants ...

This feeling of pity for the downtrodden leads him to protest, as he had done in 'Les Pauvres à l'église', about the treatment sometimes meted out to women in nineteenth-century society:

... Je vois des femmes, avec les signes du bonheur, dont, moi, j'aurais pu faire de bonnes camarades, dévorées tout d'abord par des brutes sensibles comme des bûchers ...

But despite this sympathy for women on the social level, his attitude towards them on the emotional level remains the same as in 'Les Sœurs de charité', 'Conte' and 'Génie' since he categorically states:

... Je n'aime pas les femmes. L'amour est à réinventer, on le sait.

This scarcely veiled reference to Rimbaud's homosexuality is followed by much more specific references when the 'vierge folle' talks of the 'baisers' and the 'étreintes amies' of the 'époux infernal' and describes a moment of understanding between them that is reminiscent of 'Veillées I':

... Nous nous accordions. Bien émus nous travaillions ensemble. Mais, après une pénétrante caresse, il disait: 'Comme ça te paraîtra drôle, quand je n'y serai plus, ce par quoi tu as passé. Quand tu n'auras plus mes bras sous ton cou, ni mon cœur pour t'y reposer, ni cette bouche sur tes yeux. Parce qu'il faudra que je m'en aille très loin un jour. Puis il faut que j'en aide d'autres: c'est mon devoir ...'

But the suggestion of a separation in these lines and of a duty to be accomplished indicates that Rimbaud's homosexuality was not solely a personal matter and that, as is implied in 'Chanson de la plus haute tour', 'L'Eternité' and in so many of the *Illuminations* his ambition was to change society in order to accommodate 'le nouvel amour'. This ambition is specifically referred to by the 'vierge folle' who wonders whether 'l'époux infernal' possesses 'des secrets pour changer la vie' and recognizes that this is the only alternative to moving to another country with different laws and customs:

... lui me rendra forte, nous voyagerons, nous chasserons dans les déserts, nous dormirons sur les pavés des villes inconnues, sans soins, sans peines. Ou je me réveillerai, et les lois et les mœurs auront changé, — grâce à son pouvoir magique, — le monde, en restant le même, me laissera à mes désirs, joies, nonchalances.

Implicit in this desire for change on Rimbaud's part there is the same sense of dissatisfaction with the relationship with Verlaine that is so often apparent in the *Illuminations* and it is not therefore surprising that the 'vierge folle' should also refer to another of the principle themes of the *Illuminations* and of much of Rimbaud's earlier poetry, namely his escape into the world of the imagination:

Je voyais tout le décor dont, en esprit, il s'entourait; vêtements, draps, meubles ... A côté de son cher corps endormi, que d'heures des nuits j'ai veillé, cherchant pourquoi il voulait tant s'évader de la réalité.

Not only does 'Délires I' thus paint a vivid portrait of Rimbaud, it also paints a no less vivid portrait of Verlaine, constantly stressing his extraordinary weakness of character which made him quite unable to overcome his Christian scruples about his relationship with Rimbaud and yet, at the same time, made him equally unable to break free from the latter's extraordinary power over him:

'O divin époux, mon Seigneur, ne refusez pas la confession de la plus triste de vos servantes. Je suis perdue. Je suis perdue. Je suis soûle. Je suis impure. Quelle vie!
'Pardon, divin Seigneur, pardon! Ah! pardon! Que de larmes! Et que de larmes encore plus tard, j'espère!
Plus tard, je connaîtrai le divin Epoux! Je suis née soumise à Lui. — L'autre peut me battre maintenant! ...
Je suis esclave de l'Epoux infernal, celui qui a perdu les vierges folles. C'est bien ce démon-là ... J'ai oublié tout mon devoir humain pour le suivre. Quelle vie! La vraie vie est absente. Nous ne sommes pas au monde. Je vais où il va, il le faut. Et souvent il s'emporte contre moi, *moi, la pauvre âme*.[8] Le Démon! — C'est un Démon, vous savez, *ce n'est pas un homme*.

The opposition here, in the opening lines of 'Délires I', between the 'divin époux' and the 'époux infernal' echoes the last two stanzas of Verlaine's 'Birds in the Night', written some six months before in September–October 1872 and included in *Romances sans paroles*, where he vacillates between his anxiety as a Christian and his enthusiasm as a convert to the ideas advanced by Rimbaud, whom he sees as a new Jesus with himself as the first of his disciples:[9]

> Par instants je meurs la mort du pêcheur
> Qui se sait damné s'il n'est confessé,
> Et, perdant l'espoir de nul confesseur,
> Se tord dans l'Enfer qu'il a devancé.
>
> O mais! par instants, j'ai l'extase rouge
> Du premier chrétien, sous la dent rapace,
> Qui rit à Jésus témoin, sans que bouge
> Un poil de sa chair, un nerf de sa face.

The other, related aspect of Verlaine's character that emerges from 'Délires I' is his lack of any real understanding of Rimbaud and the realization of this fact by both of them:

> . . . Hélas! je dépendais bien de lui. Mais que voulait-il avec mon existence terne et lâche? Il ne me rendait pas meilleure, s'il ne me faisait pas mourir! Tristement dépitée je lui dis quelquefois: 'Je te comprends.' Il haussait les épaules . . .
> . . . Je lui faisais promettre qu'il ne me lâcherait pas. Il l'a faite vingt fois, cette promesse d'amant. C'était aussi frivole que moi lui disant: 'Je te comprends' . . . S'il m'expliquait ses tristesses, les comprendrais-je plus que ses railleries? Il m'attaque, il passe des heures à me faire honte de tout ce qui m'a pu toucher au monde, et s'indigne si je pleure . . .

Matters had obviously deteriorated to breaking point at the time to which these words refer and it is not surprising that, looking back over the months they had managed to live together, despite the prodigious differences between them in terms of intellectual ability and strength of character, Rimbaud should have described their relationship as a 'drôle de ménage'.

'Alchimie du verbe'

The Second section of 'Délires', sub-titled 'Alchimie du verbe', is another disenchanted account of an episode now belonging to the past, but this 'histoire d'une de mes folies', as Rimbaud describes it in the opening line, is very different from the first section of 'Délires' in that it is concerned not with his moral and emotional difficulties during the preceding months but with his literary activities. A number of the poems of 1872 are quoted – or rather

misquoted, for reasons which will be explored later – as examples
of what he now regards as his foolish excursion into verbal
alchemy, namely 'Larme', 'Bonne Pensée du matin', 'Chanson de
la plus haute tour', 'Faim', 'Le loup criait', 'L'Eternité' and 'O
saisons, ô châteaux'. In between these poems Rimbaud gives a
brief and broken account of the poetic theory they are intended to
illustrate, but he does so in his usual elliptic and enigmatic
fashion so that it is not always clear what he is referring to. He
writes, for example:

> . . . J'écrivais des silences, des nuits, je notais l'inexprimable. Je
> fixais des vertiges.

He then quotes 'Larme' and 'Bonne Pensée du matin', although
nothing in either poem particularly fits this description. In the
Illuminations, however, there are several passages to which these
words could readily be applied. 'Enfance V', for example, contains a very similar phrase: 'Je suis maître du silence', and moreover, as indicated above, it paints an impressive picture of the
darkness and silence surrounding Rimbaud's basement room.
'Veillées' and 'Nocturne vulgaire' also seem to bear some relation
to Rimbaud's claim to have written about night effects, at least as
far as their titles are concerned, and several of the short passages in
'Phrases' could well be said to 'noter l'inexprimable'. As for Rimbaud's final claim: 'Je fixais des vertiges', one has only to think of
such passages as 'Mystique' or 'Being Beauteous' to appreciate
how accurately these words describe their extraordinarily dynamic
qualities.

Elsewhere in 'Délires II' Rimbaud writes:

> Je rêvais croisades, voyages de découvertes dont on n'a pas de
> relations, républiques sans histoires, guerres de religion étouffées,
> révolutions de mœurs, déplacements de races et de continents: je
> croyais à tous les enchantements.

It is true that these 'croisades' might be those of the warriors of
'Michel et Christine', mounted on their 'pâles coursiers', and that
the 'voyages de découvertes' might be an allusion to the fantastic
wanderings of 'Le Bateau ivre'. But it is equally true that 'la levée
des nouveaux hommes et leur en-marche' in 'A une Raison' could
also be one of these crusades, and that the voyages of discovery
could refer to 'Mouvement' whose 'voyageurs' set off 'dans
l'héroïsme de la découverte'. Similarly the 'républiques sans histoires' may refer to Rimbaud's dream of destroying the 'répub-

liques de ce monde' in 'Qu'est-ce pour nous' and the 'guerres de religion étouffées' may refer to the 'religieuse après-midi d'orage' that sweeps over Europe in 'Michel et Christine'. But again it is equally true that these phrases also call to mind such passages as 'Démocratie', 'Guerre' and 'Soir historique' in the *Illuminations*. As for the 'révolutions de mœurs' of which Rimbaud dreamed, these call to mind very strongly indeed the 'révolutions de l'amour' in 'Conte', just as the 'déplacements de races' echo the 'migrations plus énormes que les anciennes invasions' of 'Génie', and the 'déplacement de continents', the cosmic destruction visualized towards the end of 'Soir historique'.

A little later in 'Délires II' Rimbaud returns to this idea that he had lived in a dream world with the words: 'Je m'habituai à l'hallucination simple', a statement which may well be a less vivid and less immediate version of the last of the short passages in 'Phrases':

> Je baisse les feux du lustre, je me jette sur le lit, et, tourné du côté de l'ombre, je vous vois, mes filles! mes reines!

He then goes on to give examples of these hallucinations to which he became accustomed. 'Je voyais très franchement une mosquée à la place d'une usine' is the first of these examples, but since it does not actually exist anywhere in Rimbaud's work it is clearly meant as a specimen of the kind of imaginative transformation to which he subjected the world around him. It is true that, as has been shown throughout the preceding pages, this is a constant feature of Rimbaud's work, but it is also true that some of the re-creative passages in the *Illuminations* spring particularly to mind in this connection, especially 'Villes I' where the substitution of a palm tree for a lamp-post and of a 'boulevard de Bagdad' for a London street offer close parallels to the substitution of a mosque for a factory. Similarly Rimbaud's claim to have seen 'les monstres, les mystères' could refer to the exotic sea creatures encountered by 'Le Bateau ivre' in its mysterious voyages, but it could equally well refer to the fantasy figures in 'Antique' and 'Being Beauteous' and to such mysterious scenes as the one depicted in 'Parade' which ends with Rimbaud's statement that he alone holds the key to the mystery: 'J'ai seul la clef de cette parade sauvage'.

In the case of these examples it does therefore seem that Rimbaud may be referring to his imaginative powers both in his earlier poetry and in the *Illuminations*. But in the case of another

example of the kind of hallucinations to which he became accustomed: '[Je voyais] un salon au fond d'un lac', there seems to be
so clear an echo of a phrase in 'Soir historique': 'On joue aux
cartes au fond de l'étang', that it is difficult to deny that he must
have been thinking solely and specifically of this particular
passage.

Yet although Rimbaud thus seems to be including the *Illuminations* along with his earlier poetry as part of the foolish excursion
into verbal alchemy which he now deplores, he does not quote a
single passage from the *Illuminations* alongside the seven poems of
1872 that are so extensively quoted. This is obviously a strong
argument against the suggestion that 'Délires II' refers in part to
the *Illuminations* and consequently against the belief that the latter
were written before *Une Saison en enfer*. It should be noted, however, that Rimbaud is clearly quoting his poems from memory
and thus makes a considerable number of mistakes. The second
and third stanzas of 'Larme', for example, are imperfectly recol-
lected and the final quatrain has disappeared altogether save for a
single line very different from the original. Only two of the
original six stanzas of 'Chanson de la plus haute tour' are quoted
and the refrain contains an unwarranted subjunctive resulting
from the fact that Rimbaud has remembered the rhyme but not
the way he arrived at it:

> Qu'il vienne, qu'il vienne
> Le temps dont on s'éprenne.

Two of the stanzas of 'L'Eternité' are switched round, the regular
five syllable rhythm of the earlier version is interrupted on three
occasions by four syllable lines being substituted instead, and a
number of the lines are poorly remembered. The sixth couplet of
'O saisons, ô châteaux' has been completely forgotten and the
eighth couplet, crossed out on the original manuscript, has been
quoted, or misquoted, in its stead. If Rimbaud could not therefore remember accurately the poems he had written twelve
months before, despite the aids to memory that rhyme and
rhythm undoubtedly constitute, it is perhaps not so surprising
that none of the prose passages of the *Illuminations* should be
quoted in 'Délires II' and that he should have preferred to define
the methods he had used rather than to quote the results.

But although no actual passage from the *Illuminations* is to be
found in 'Délires II', a short passage in prose is nevertheless

quoted that reads very much like the beginning of one of Rimbaud's prose poems:

> 'Genéral, s'il reste un vieux canon sur tes remparts en ruines, bombarde-nous avec des blocs de terre sèche. Aux glaces des magasins splendides! dans les salons! Fais manger sa poussière à la ville. Oxyde les gargouilles. Emplis les boudoirs de poudre de rubis brûlante . . .'

Such exclamatory commands are typical of several passages of the *Illuminations* – 'Gracieux fils de Pan . . . promène-toi la nuit' ('Antique'); 'Ecume, roule sur le pont et par-dessus les bois' ('Après le déluge'); 'Aux pays poivrés et détrempés!' ('Démocratie'); 'Arrière ces superstitions!' ('Génie'); 'Change nos lots, crible les fléaux' ('A une raison'). As for the vocabulary, it is a curious fact that most of the words in this prose passage can be found in the *Illuminations* – 'général', 'vieux', 'remparts' and 'terre' all occur within the space of a few lines in 'Enfance II' which goes on to describe a dilapidated castle, even though the words 'en ruines' are not actually used; 'canon' occurs in 'Being Beauteous'; 'glaces' in 'Après le déluge', 'Nocturne vulgaire', 'Métropolitain' and 'Dévotion'; 'salon' in 'Enfance V' and 'Scènes'; 'gargouille' in 'Nocturne vulgaire'; 'poudre' in 'Phrases' and 'rubis' in 'Fleurs'. Most significant of all, the passage has that surreal quality that characterizes so many of the *Illuminations*, with the logic of the opening words disintegrating as the sentences follow one another. It does therefore seem possible that in this quotation Rimbaud may be making up a specimen passage typical of the *Illuminations* to illustrate the kind of prose writing in which he had engaged after the free verse poems of 1872.

All such participation in experimental writing appears now, however, to be dismissed in peremptory fashion in the final line of 'Délires II' in favour of a passive recognition of the virtues of more formal qualities:

> Cela s'est passé, je sais aujourd'hui saluer la beauté.

A somewhat longer phrase towards the end of the rough draft of 'Délires II' seems to confirm this interpretation:

> Je hais maintenant les élans mystiques et les bizarreries de style. Maintenant je puis dire que l'art est une sottise.

But although the phrase 'les élans mystiques et les bizarreries de style' seems to be an excellent definition not only of such poems as

'L'Eternité', 'Larme' and 'O Saisons, ô châteaux' but also of such prose passages as 'Mystique', 'Matinée d'ivresse', 'Barbare' and 'Génie', and although the phrase 'l'art est une sottise' appears to mean that Rimbaud has decided to give up writing altogether, such an interpretation assumes that Rimbaud had already written the *Illuminations* before 1873 and that after that date he gave up all forms of literary activity. Those who believe that some of the *Illuminations* were written after *Une Saison en enfer* are therefore obliged to interpret the final lines of 'Délires II' and of the rough draft in a very different sense and to argue, as does Suzanne Bernard,[10] that Rimbaud is not bidding farewell to all literary activity and that, moreover, it is solely the poetry of 1872 that is to be equated with the 'art' which he now dismisses and with 'les élans mystiques et les bizarreries de style' which he now rejects. But if this is the case, it is difficult to see how Rimbaud could then have proceeded to write the *Illuminations* which, as has been shown above, are a natural extension of the 'vers nouveaux' of 1872. One would have expected him, on the contrary, to revert to the kind of poetry, conventional in both form and content, that he had written in 1870 and 1871, such as 'Le Dormeur du val' and 'Les Sœurs de charité'. It is interesting, in this connection, to note that Verlaine, whose poetry in 1872 and early 1873 kept pace with that of Rimbaud and became much more free than it had been hitherto, reverted to a more formal kind of style once the episode with Rimbaud was over.[11]

The pursuit of happiness

Rimbaud's dismissal, in the two sections of 'Délires', of his life with Verlaine and of his poetic experiments of 1872–3 is parallelled, in the rest of *Une Saison en enfer*, by his dismissal of other aspects of his revolt against society.

After a short preface, almost certainly written after the Brussels incident, introducing 'ces quelques hideux feuillets de mon carnet de damné', he begins by describing and justifying his one-time attitude in the long first chapter, 'Mauvais sang', which is in the present tense, either because Rimbaud wanted to make his account more vivid, or because this chapter was written early enough for him still not to have entirely rejected his ideas, that is to say in late April or early May 1873, before the final break with Verlaine. The particular theme to which he constantly returns is that he does not belong to modern civilization but that he is a kind of throw-back to a pre-Christian era. From the very first line he stresses the fact that he is descended from the Gauls and possesses both their physical and their mental characteristics:

> J'ai de mes ancêtres gaulois l'œil bleu et blanc, la cervelle étroite et la maladresse dans la lutte . . .
> D'eux, j'ai: l'idolâtrie et l'amour du sacrilège; —oh! tous les vices, colère, luxure,—magnifique, la luxure;—surtout mensonge et paresse.

At the beginning of the second of the eight sections into which 'Mauvais sang' is divided, he denies that he has any links with France after the period of the Gauls and insists that he has always belonged to a different race:

> Si j'avais des antécédents à un point quelconque de l'histoire de France!
> Mais non, rien.
> Il m'est bien évident que j'ai toujours été race inférieure . . .

This expression about belonging to a 'race inférieure' is repeated on two further occasions in the second section and the similar idea of having in one's veins the 'mauvais sang' of the title is repeated when Rimbaud states, in the third section, that, despite the advent of Christianity, 'le sang païen revient'. He feels a certain regret that he is therefore excluded from the Christian community, but he is also determined that his 'race inférieure' will one day be transformed into a 'race forte' and that he himself will no longer be an outcast:

> Ma journée est faite; je quitte l'Europe. L'air marin brûlera mes poumons; les climats perdus me tanneront . . .
> Je reviendrai avec des membres de fer, la peau sombre, l'œil furieux: sur mon masque, on me jugera d'une race forte . . .

These optimistic lines are followed, in the fourth section, by a sudden realization that such a transformation is not easy and that for the present he is a prisoner in an alien society, bearing the mark of a vice which remains unspecified but which most commentators agree must refer to his homosexuality:

> On ne part pas. Reprenons le chemin d'ici, chargé de mon vice, le vice qui a poussé ses racines de souffrance à mon côté dès l'âge de raison—qui monte au ciel, me bat, me renverse, me traîne . . .

This interpretation seems to be confirmed by Rimbaud's frank

statement in the fifth section that 'l'orgie et la camaraderie des
femmes m'étaient interdites' which leads into a renewed insistence
on his paganism:

> ... Je n'ai jamais été de ce peuple-ci; je n'ai jamais été chrétien; je
> suis de la race qui chantait dans le supplice; je ne comprends pas les
> lois; je n'ai pas le sens moral, je suis une brute ...

But instead of associating himself with a people outside Christianity in terms of time, he now sees himself as belonging to a race
outside Christianity in terms of space:

> Oui, j'ai les yeux fermés à votré lumière. Je suis une bête, un
> nègre ...

If he is a 'negro' however, so too, under their veneer of Christianity, are the members of western civilization:

> ... Marchand, tu es nègre; magistrat, tu es nègre; général, tu es
> nègre ...

He again feels the longing to leave Europe for the 'vrai royaume
des enfants de Cham', tempted by the primitive quality of life
there: 'Faim, soif, cris, danse, danse, danse, danse!'.

But just as his previous departure was suddenly halted, so too
this dream of a new life is abruptly destroyed at the beginning of
the sixth section by the invading forces of white civilization:

> Les blancs débarquent. Le canon! Il faut se soumettre au baptême,
> s'habiller, travailler.

Rimbaud appears to yield to the pressures to which he is thus subjected and the sixth section ends with a temporary return to the
Christian faith:

> La raison m'est née. Le monde est bon. Je bénirai la vie. J'aimerai
> mes frères. Ce ne sont plus des promesses d'enfance. Ni l'espoir
> d'échapper à la vieillesse et à la mort. Dieu fait ma force, et je loue
> Dieu.

This feeling of salvation and of having put behind him his
recent past is continued at the beginning of the seventh section:

> L'ennui n'est plus mon amour. Les rages, les débauches, la folie,
> dont je sais tous les élans et les désastres,—tout mon fardeau est
> déposé. Apprécions sans vertige l'étendue de mon innocence.

He no longer takes any comfort from being at odds with the world:

> Je ne serais plus capable de demander le réconfort d'une baston-
> nade.

Nor is his Christianity of a purely sentimental nature:

> . . . Je ne me crois pas embarqué pour une noce avec Jésus-Christ
> pour beau-père.

On the other hand, however, he has no wish to remain a prisoner of his rediscovered faith: 'Je veux la liberté dans le salut'. This phrase marks a new direction in Rimbaud's thoughts as the attractions of a quietly Christian way of life begin to fade:

> Quant au bonheur établi, domestique ou non . . . non, je ne peux
> pas. Je suis trop dissipé, trop faible.

The section then ends with Rimbaud spurning the innocence that he has just begun to appreciate and returning to his mood of cynical contempt for life:

> . . . Mon innocence me ferait pleurer. La vie est la farce à mener par
> tous.

His hope of salvation and his prospect of returning to the Christian community has thus been quickly dispelled and the eighth and final section of 'Mauvais sang' conjures up, in a few vivid and staccato phrases, the image of punishment as an alternative means by which he can be brought back to what he sarcastically calls, in an echo of the 'gaulois' theme of the beginning of the chapter, 'la vie française, le sentier de l'honneur'.

The second chapter, 'Nuit de l'enfer', resembles 'Mauvais sang' in that it too deals with the theme of Christianity and paganism, but Rimbaud's attitude has now changed and instead of emphasizing that he does not belong to the Christian community, he stresses, on the contrary, the fact that he cannot escape from it:

> . . . Je suis esclave de mon baptême. Parents, vous avez fait mon
> malheur et vous avec fait le vôtre. Pauvre innocent! L'enfer ne peut
> attaquer les païens.

Consequently the dream of abolishing the distinction between good and evil to which he had referred in 'Matinée d'ivresse' and to which Verlaine was to refer in 'Crimen amoris' is now over:

> J'avais entrevu la conversion au bien et au bonheur, le salut.
> Puis-je décrire le vision, l'air de l'enfer ne souffre pas les hymnes!
> C'était des millions de créatures charmantes, un suave concert
> spirituel, la force et la paix, les nobles ambitions, que sais-je? Les
> nobles ambitions!

The 'poison' of the 'lettre du voyant' and 'Matinée d'ivresse'
which was ultimately to have had beneficial results, is now seen to
have had no such effect. On the contrary, the torture through
which Rimbaud was to have passed to reach his state of bliss has
now been revealed as endless:

> J'ai avalé une fameuse gorgée de poison.—Trois fois béni soit le
> conseil qui m'est arrivé!—Les entrailles me brûlent. La violence du
> venin tord mes membres, me rend difforme, me terrasse. Je meurs
> de soif, j'étouffe, je ne puis crier. C'est l'enfer, l'éternelle peine!

He recognizes that his inordinate ambition to reform the world
sprang from a pride and vanity which he now mocks:

> . . . Je suis maître en fantasmagories.
> Ecoutez!
> J'ai tous les talents . . .

He parodies his former vision of himself as a new Christ:

> Fiez-vous donc à moi, la foi soulage, guide, guérit. Tous, venez,—
> même les petits enfants,—que je vous console, qu'on répande pour
> vous son cœur,—le cœur merveilleux!—Pauvres hommes, travail-
> leurs! Je ne demande pas de prières; avec votre confiance seulement
> je serai heureux.

He now acknowledges that his dream of a 'conversion au bien et
au bonheur' was a 'fausse conversion' to use the abandoned title of
the first draft of this chapter and that he has, on the contrary, been
plunged into the 'nuit de l'enfer' of the final title.

Like the second chapter, the fourth chapter, 'L'Impossible', as the
title implies, is concerned with the reasons why Rimbaud found it
impossible to achieve his goal and once again he emphasizes the
fact that he does not by nature belong to western civilization:

> . . . Je vois que mes malaises viennent de ne m'être pas figuré assez
> tôt que nous sommes à l'Occident . . . J'envoyais au diable les palmes
> des martyrs, les rayons de l'art, l'orgueil des inventeurs, l'ardeur des
> pillards; je retournais à l'Orient et à la sagesse première et éternelle.

But his refusal to conform to conventional opinion in matters of religion, aesthetics, scientific discoveries and commercial exploitation meant that the kind of life he led was dismissed as 'un rêve de paresse grossière'.

There is, however, one way out of the difficulty faced by someone who feels alienated from the world around him: 'Vous êtes en Occident mais libre d'habiter dans votre Orient'. That is to say that the era of primitive innocence to which Rimbaud wants to return, the garden of Eden he is looking for, in short the kind of God that he is seeking, can be found through a life of the mind, irrespective of material surroundings. It is this realization which leads him to declare, at the end of the chapter: 'Par l'esprit on va à Dieu', and to describe as a 'déchirante infortune' the fact that this realization has come so late.

In one of those sudden changes of direction that characterize *Une Saison en enfer*, the fifth chapter, 'L'Eclair', abruptly proposes an alternative route towards the new world that Rimbaud wants:

> Le travail humain! c'est l'explosion qui éclaire mon abîme de temps en temps.

But he rejects this solution as quickly as the related alternative of progress through science: 'Je connais le travail et la science est trop lente'. This leads into a moment of extreme pessimism:

> Ma vie est usée. Allons! feignons, fainéantons, ô pitié! Et nous existerons en nous amusant, en rêvant amours monstres et univers fantastiques.

In what is almost certainly an allusion to the brief period he spent in hospital in Brussels after the shooting incident of July 1873, he moves towards accepting the idea of death as a means of escape:

> Sur mon lit d'hôpital, l'odeur de l'encens m'est revenue si puissante; gardien des aromates sacrés, confesseur, martyr . . .

But his fundamentally rebellious nature brusquely erupts again:

> Je reconnais là ma sale éducation d'enfance. Puis quoi! . . . Aller mes vingt ans, si les autres vont vingt ans . . .
> Non! non! à présent je me révolte contre la mort!

He seems therefore determined to continue his life as an outcast in society, even if this means that the new era that he longs for will never be reached:

> Alors,—oh!—chère pauvre âme, l'éternité serait-elle pas perdue
> pour nous!

With this question at the end of the fifth chapter Rimbaud plumbs
the depths of despair in *Une Saison en enfer*. In the sixth chapter,
'Matin', he recognizes that he has no more to say about his
situation and his past experiences:

> Pourtant, aujourd'hui, je crois avoir fini la relation de mon enfer.
> C'était bien l'enfer; l'ancien, celui dont le fils de l'homme ouvrit
> les portes.

This sentence clearly links up with the reference in 'Nuit de l'enfer'
to pagans being free from the idea of hell and with the general
theme of the previous chapters that Rimbaud is an outcast from
the Christian community. But the previous chapters have also
shown his stubborn refusal to surrender and once again he looks
forward to the advent of the new era he is seeking:

> . . . Quand irons-nous, par-delà les grèves et les monts, saluer la
> naissance du travail nouveau, la sagesse nouvelle, la fuite des tyrans
> et des démons, la fin de la superstition, adorer—les premiers! Noël
> sur la terre!
> Le chant des cieux, la marche des peuples! Esclaves, ne maudis-
> sons pas la vie.

In the final chapter, appropriately entitled 'Adieu', this mixture
of optimism and pessimism continues as Rimbaud reflects that,
although autumn, with all its symbolic significance,[12] was drawing
near as he was completing *Une Saison en enfer*, he has no need to
regret the darkening days since he is seeking a spiritual rather than
a physical source of light:

> L'automne déjà!—Mais pourquoi regretter un éternel soleil, si
> nous sommes engagés à la découverte de la clarté divine,—loin des
> gens qui meurent sur les saisons.

But the thought of autumn and more particularly, no doubt, of
the previous autumn of 1872 when he and Verlaine had set sail
from Ostend for Dover on 7 September on the way to London,
leads to a paragraph full of darkness and bitterness as he recalls
that unhappy period:

> L'automne. Notre barque élevée dans les brumes immobiles
> tourne vers le port de la misère, la cité énorme au ciel taché de feu et

de boue. Ah! les haillons pourris, le pain trempé de pluie, l'ivresse, les mille amours qui m'ont crucifié!

These sombre reflections on the past are, however, counterbalanced by a radiant picture of the promised land and by a series of comments on his past achievements which seem to define with a remarkable accuracy certain passages of the *Illuminations*:

— Quelquefois je vois au ciel des plages sans fin couvertes de blanches nations en joie. Un grand vaisseau d'or, au-dessus de moi, agite ses pavillons multicolores sous les brises du matin. J'ai créé toutes les fêtes, tous les triomphes, tous les drames. J'ai essayé d'inventer de nouvelles fleurs, de nouveaux astres, de nouvelles chairs, de nouvelles langues. J'ai cru acquérir des pouvoirs surnaturels . . . [13]

But again the plunge into pessimism occurs as he realizes that all this creative activity, not only in the realm of literature but also in the realm of ideas, is now ended:

. . . Eh bien! je dois enterrer mon imagination et mes souvenirs. Une belle gloire de conteur et d'artiste emportée!

Moi! moi qui me suis dit mage ou ange, dispensé de toute morale, je suis rendu au sol, avec un devoir à chercher, et la réalité rugueuse à étreindre. Paysan!

Furthermore, not only have all his high hopes been dashed, but he now feels, after the break with Verlaine, entirely alone with no one to help him out of his difficulties:

Mais pas une main amie! et où puiser le secours?

Yet despite this feeling of failure and solitude, he paradoxically claims, in the final paragraphs of *Une Saison en enfer*, that he has won a kind of victory in the sense that he has now recovered from his anger, regret and grief at what has occurred and can put all this past history behind him:

Car je puis dire que la victoire m'est acquise: les grincements de dents, les sifflements de feu, les soupirs empestés se modèrent. Tous les souvenirs immondes s'effacent. Mes derniers regrets détalent . . .

This leads into another radiant picture of the promised land that he feels convinced will one day be reached:

. . . Recevons tous les influx de vigueur et de tendresse réelle. Et à l'aurore, armés d'une ardente patience, nous entrerons aux splendides villes.

As for the means by which it is to be attained, Rimbaud's conclusion, in the last paragraph of *Une Saison en enfer*, is that he no longer believes in the concept of 'l'amour universel'. His solitude no longer appears to him as a cause for complaint:

> Que parlais-je de main amie! Un bel avantage, c'est que je puis rire des vieilles amours mensongères, et frapper de honte ces couples menteurs . . .

There can be little doubt that these lines refer to the relationship with Verlaine, despite the fact that Rimbaud then adds the somewhat surprising phrase: 'J'ai vu l'enfer des femmes là-bas'. Suzanne Bernard suggests that this may be a reference to the 'vierge folle', but it may also be an admission by Rimbaud that he does not regard heterosexuality as an alternative to homosexuality but simply as another aspect of 'l'amour universel' which must therefore be rejected so that he can pursue his own solitary path towards true happiness:

> . . . et il me sera loisible de *posséder la vérité dans une âme et un corps.*

Old and new techniques

If *Une Saison en enfer* is an account of the new attitudes Rimbaud adopted in the summer of 1873 towards the three-fold ambition he had once had of forging a lasting relationship with Verlaine, of writing a new kind of poetry and of reforming the moral basis on which western society is founded, it is only to be expected that this rejection of his earlier ideas should be expressed in ways very different from those which he had previously used and which are condemned with such scorn in 'Alchimie du verbe'. One immediately obvious difference is that *Une Saison en enfer* is very much a prose work and although, on occasions, there are passages that have a poetic quality, such as the lines at the end of 'Matin' looking forward to the advent of a new era, or the sombre opening paragraphs of 'Adieu', recalling the despondent weeks in London, or the later paragraph of 'Adieu' painting a radiant picture of the promised land, on the whole Rimbaud seems to make little or no attempt to achieve the poetic effects that have been analysed in the *Illuminations*. On the contrary, he not infrequently lapses into language of a clumsy banality, as when he writes, in 'Mauvais sang':

... C'est très-certain, c'est oracle, ce que je dis. Je comprends, et ne sachant m'expliquer sans paroles païennes, je voudrais me taire;

or as when he writes in 'L'Impossible':

Mes deux sous de raison sont finis!—L'esprit est autorité. Il veut que je sois en Occident. Il faudrait le faire taire pour conclure comme je voulais.

Not only does *Une Saison en enfer* thus use language for the purpose of 'reportage' as Mallarmé put it, rather than for the purpose of poetry, but it also, in consequence, abandons, for the most part, the idea advanced in the 'lettre du voyant' that the poet is a passive instrument played upon by outside forces. The first section of 'Délires' in particular is far removed from such free-flowing passages as 'Barbare' and 'Ville' and such inconsequential poems as 'Chant de guerre parisien' and 'Entends comme brame'. The technique of ostensibly quoting the 'vierge folle' who, in turn, ostensibly quotes the 'époux infernal' is clearly a complex one that cannot have sprung from any 'désordre de l'esprit' but must, on the contrary, have resulted from a conscious control as rigorous as in such conventional poems of 1870 and 1871 as 'Le Forgeron' and 'Les Premières Communions'. The second section of 'Délires' too is coherently organized and pursues a clear line of argument as Rimbaud amplifies his opening statement that he is going to recount 'l'histoire d'une de mes folies', even if the poems he quotes do not always illustrate his points particularly well.

The remaining chapters of *Une Saison en enfer*, as has just been shown, also pursue a theme to which Rimbaud constantly returns, developing successive stages in his argument so as to arrive at his conclusion. But in matters of detail these chapters are much less carefully ordered than the two sections of 'Délires' and they frequently give the impression that Rimbaud is allowing his thoughts to stray from the essential point, distracted by associated ideas and images. In the opening lines of 'Mauvais sang' for example, his contention that he is descended from the Gauls leads him to drift into details about them that are irrelevant to his argument:

J'ai de mes ancêtres gaulois l'œil bleu blanc, la cervelle étroite, et la maladresse dans la lutte. Je trouve mon habillement aussi barbare que le leur. Mais je ne beurre pas ma chevelure.

Les Gaulois étaient des écorcheurs de bêtes, les brûleurs d'herbes les plus ineptes de leur temps . . .

Towards the end of the same chapter Rimbaud's lack of conscious control over what Suzanne Bernard calls 'ce texte chaotique' takes a different form as he vividly but far from coherently conveys his sense of being forced, like an unwilling conscript, to fight for a cause he does not support:

> Assez! voici la punition. *En marche*!
> Ah! les poumons brûlent, les tempes grondent! la nuit roule dans mes yeux, par ce soleil! le cœur . . . les membres . . .
> Où va-t-on? au combat? Je suis faible! les autres avancent. Les outils, les armes . . . le temps!
> Feu! feu sur moi! Là ou je me rends.—Lâches!—Je me tue! Je me jette aux pieds des chevaux!
> Ah! . . .
> —Je m'y habituerai.
> Ce serait la vie francaise, le sentier de l'honneur!

This kind of style, strongly reminiscent of such texts as 'L'Orgie parisienne' and 'Démocratie', is to be found in other chapters of *Une Saison en enfer* where Rimbaud allows his thoughts and feelings to pour out, as in the following paragraph from 'Nuit de l'enfer':

> Tais-toi, mais tais-toi! . . . C'est la honte, le reproche, ici: Satan qui dit que le feu est ignoble, que ma colère est affreusement sotte.—Assez! . . . Des erreurs qu'on me souffle, magies, parfums faux, musiques puériles.—Et dire que je tiens la vérité, que je vois la justice: j'ai un jugement sain et arrêté, jé suis prêt pour la perfection . . . Orgueil.—La peau de ma tête se dessèche. Pitié! Seigneur, j'ai peur. J'ai soif, si soif! Ah! l'enfance, l'herbe, la pluie, le lac sur les pierres, *le clair de lune quand le clocher sonnait douze* . . . le diable est au clocher, à cette heure. Marie! Sainte-Vierge! . . .—Horreur de ma bêtise.

In 'L'Impossible' too, despite the fact that the general theme of the chapter is fairly clear, there are many passages where Rimbaud's ideas appear to have run away with him so that the reader is left far behind, as in the following paragraph:

> Hier encore je soupirais: 'Ciel! sommes-nous assez de damnés ici-bas! Moi j'ai tant de temps déjà dans leur troupe. Je les connais tous. Nous nous reconnaissons toujours; nous nous dégoûtons. La charité nous est inconnue. Mais nous sommes polis, nos relations avec le monde sont très-convenables'. Est-ce étonnant? Le monde! les marchands, les naïfs! —Nous ne sommes pas déshonorés.—Mais les élus, comment nous recevraient-ils? Or il y a des gens hargneux

et joyeux, de faux élus, puisqu'il nous faut de l'audace ou de l'humilité pour les aborder. Ce sont les seuls élus. Ce ne sont pas des bénisseurs!

If the two sections of 'Délires' are as carefully composed as the conventional poems of 1870 and 1871, the remaining chapters of *Une Saison en enfer* may therefore be compared to 'Le Bateau ivre' and other poems of late 1871 in that, although they have a fairly clear overall pattern, within this framework there is evidence of a decided 'désordre de l'esprit'. The Rimbaud of the 'lettre du voyant' thus still persists in *Une Saison en enfer*, standing aside on occasions and allowing his thoughts and feelings to unfold; but the earlier Rimbaud of the period before the 'lettre du voyant' has begun to re-assert his authority, ordering every detail of the two sections of 'Délires' and consciously shaping the outline of the other chapters so that their logical train of thought, however much it may be interrupted, is never entirely lost.[14]

VI

AFTER *UNE SAISON EN ENFER*

The fact that, in *Une Saison en enfer*, Rimbaud abandons his desire to create a new kind of world and a new kind of poetry and that, in so doing, he begins to move away from his 'désordre de l'esprit' towards more orderly modes of expression is a powerful argument, as has been noted earlier, in support of the belief that, had he continued to write poetry after 1873, he could not have written the prose poems of the *Illuminations* but would have returned to the kind of verse he had written in 1870 and 1871.

But if it therefore seems probable that, after *Une Saison en enfer*, Rimbaud lapsed into silence, this is not to say that he completely withdrew his violent criticism of the world in which he lived. The enigmatic final lines of *Une Saison en enfer* seem to announce a new phase in Rimbaud's revolt. He no longer believes in the doctrine of 'l'amour universel' and no longer intends to play the rôle of 'le plus beau d'entre tous les mauvais anges' of Verlaine's 'Crimen amoris', leading a crusade for the liberation of mankind from the concept of sin. This does not mean, however, that he was to follow Verlaine in recognizing the error of his ways and in repenting for his sins by returning to the Christian faith. It is interesting, in this connection, to note that, in a letter dated 12 December 1875, Verlaine clearly felt that Rimbaud was ready for the same conversion to Christianity that he himself had recently experienced: 'Ce m'est un si grand chagrin de te voir en tes voies idiotes, toi si intelligent, si *prêt* (bien que ça puisse t'étonner!). J'en appelle à ton dégoût lui-même de tout et de tous, à ta perpétuelle colère contre chaque chose—juste, au fond, cette colère, bien qu'inconscient du *pourquoi*'. But Rimbaud was made of sterner stuff than his former 'compagnon d'enfer' and, although defeated, he refused, in the final paragraphs of *Une Saison en enfer* to concede victory to the forces that had crushed him. His policy now was to opt out of society in his vagabond years as 'l'homme aux semelles de vent' from 1875 to 1880 and finally to turn his back on Europe so as to live, from 1880 to 1890, in Aden and Harar.

Whether he remained a defeated but unrepentant rebel to the bitter end depends on how one interprets the controversial episode of his deathbed conversion. There is clearly a case to be made for dismissing it as no more than an empty gesture devoid of any real significance. But there is equally clearly a case to be made for accepting it as a long-delayed response to Verlaine's perceptive comment and for believing that Rimbaud finally came to acknowledge that he was an ally rather than an enemy of Christianity in his 'dégoût de tout et de tous', in his 'perpétuelle colère contre chaque chose' and in his resolve that 'à l'aurore, armés d'une ardente patience, nous entrerons aux splendides villes'.

NOTES AND REFERENCES

Details as to the publisher and the date and place of publication of works listed in the bibliography are not repeated here.

I. THE BIOGRAPHICAL BACKGROUND

1. See the letter dated 24 September 1870 in Arthur Rimbaud, *Oeuvres complètes*, ed. Antoine Adam, 1972, p. 244. All items of Rimbaud's correspondence mentioned in the course of the present study can be found in this edition which will be referred to as *O.C. 1972*.

2. See the 'lettre de protestation' drawn up by Rimbaud and sent to the Mayor of Douai by the local contingent of the National Guard and the minutes of an election meeting also drawn up by Rimbaud in *O.C. 1972*, pp. 241–3.

3. See *O.C. 1972*, p. 889.

4. See C. Chadwick, *Verlaine*, 'Athlone French Poets' The Athlone Press, University of London, 1973, pp. 3 and 123.

5. See *O.C. 1972*, pp. 822–33.

6. For details of these and other aspects of Rimbaud's life see *O.C. 1972*, pp. xxxix–lii.

7. See *O.C. 1972*, pp. 302–3 and the note on p. 1096–7.

8. Rimbaud kept a diary of this agonisingly painful journey – see *O.C. 1972*, pp. 659–61.

9. See *O.C. 1972*, pp. 698–707.

II. THE EARLY POETRY: 1870–1871

1. Antoine Adam, in *O.C. 1972*, pp. 891–2, adopts the suggestion made by M. Ruff in his *Rimbaud*, pp. 58–9, that 'L'Orgie parisienne' is concerned with the return to Paris, not of those who fled during the Commune but of those who had fled earlier during the Franco-Prussian war. M. Ruff thus discounts the date of May 1871 attributed to the poem in the version printed in *La Plume* in 1890 and in the *Poésies complètes* of 1895. He prefers to date the poem from the time of Rimbaud's third 'fugue' at the end of February and the beginning of March 1871 when the armistice between France and Prussia which had been signed on 28 January and the peace terms which were ratified by the National Assembly on 1 March encouraged the people of Paris to return to their homes.

2. See Suzanne Bernard, ed., *Oeuvres*, p. 450, note 5.

3. See *O.C. 1972*, p. 1022, note 3.

4. It must be made clear that this reading of the concluding stanzas of

'Le Bateau ivre' is very different from the one that is generally accepted. The conventional interpretation of the poem does not recognize that the essential theme of the final stanza is a refusal to follow a fixed course and, by implication, a complementary desire to drift freely along. On the contrary, these lines are usually interpreted as expressing a refusal to engage any longer in the kind of voyages that have been described earlier in the poem. Consequently, 'Le Bateau ivre' is generally thought of as a poem of depression and despair, with the cry: 'O que ma quille éclate!' being understood as a wish for self-destruction. This reading, however, does not take account of the succeeding cry: 'O que j'aille à la mer!' which can only mean that the vessel wishes to put to sea again – by no stretch of the imagination can 'aller à la mer' mean 'to sink', as Antoine Adam suggests in *O.C. 1972*, p. 924. These two apparently contradictory exclamations can in fact be reconciled if it is appreciated that the bursting of the keel will not destroy the vessel but will simply restore it to its earlier condition of a leaking hulk, as described in line 18: 'L'eau verte pénétra ma coque de sapin'. It should also be noted that the conventional interpretation ignores the biographical circumstances in which 'Le Bateau ivre' was written, when Rimbaud was about to break out of Charleville once more in another attempt to explore wider horizons, not when he was about to abandon his desire for freedom and accept the restrictions of life in the quiet backwater of the Ardennes. The present author has long been convinced that the superficial equation of the sea imagery in the final stanza with the sea imagery in the earlier stanzas has led to a widespread and persistent misunderstanding of the meaning of the poem – see C. Chadwick, 'Le sens du *Bateau ivre*' in the *Revue d'Histoire Littéraire de la France*, 1958, pp. 528–32, and the consequent exchange of letters with Suzanne Bernard in the *R.H.L.F.*, 1959, pp. 569–72. See also C. Chadwick, *Etudes sur Rimbaud*, pp. 20–6.

5. It should be remembered that 'assister à' means 'to be present at', not 'to assist'.

6. It should be noted that on the manuscript of 'Chant de guerre parisien' Rimbaud writes in the margin: 'Quelles rimes! O quelles rimes!'

7. See *O.C. 1972*, pp. 899–901 for a summary of several of these interpretations.

8. See C. Chadwick, 'Rimbaud le poète' in the *R.H.L.F.*, 1960, pp. 204–11, and C. Chadwick, *Etudes sur Rimbaud*, pp. 27–40.

9. There is no justification for Antoine Adam's assumption that 'Banville répondit à cette lettre mais sa réponse est perdue' (*O.C. 1972*, p. 1068).

III. THE LATER POETRY: 1871–1872

1. As has been frequently pointed out, there is no such animal as a 'Rocky Mountain cat', but the following line makes it clear that Rimbaud was thinking of a skunk, known in French as a 'putois d'Amérique',

for which 'chat des Monts-Rocheux' is a reasonable equivalent, given the necessity of finding a rhyme for 'Dieu'. If Rimbaud knew the alternative name of 'polecat' this too could have helped him in his choice of words.

2. According to Antoine Adam, *O.C. 1972*, p. 943: '*Lui*, c'est naturellement Rimbaud'; but this hasty assumption ignores the fact that the function of the word 'lui' here clearly seems to be to distinguish between two different people. If the rest of the poem is concerned with Rimbaud, as Adam agrees, then the 'lui' must surely refer to someone else, presumably Verlaine.

3. Various dates have been suggested for Rimbaud's return to Charleville in the spring of 1872. Verlaine's letter to him dated 2 April discusses the removal of his belongings from his lodgings in the Rue Campagne Première, rented 'jusqu'au huit'. Rimbaud must therefore have left Paris shortly before, but sufficiently long before to have had an exchange of letters with Verlaine, since the latter mentions the receipt of an earlier letter from Rimbaud and refers to a letter of his own that he had sent in reply: 'Et merci pour ta bonne lettre . . . Tu as dû ailleurs depuis recevoir ma lettre sur pelure rose, et probablement m'y répondre'. It seems reasonable to allow about a week for this exchange of letters and to calculate therefore that Rimbaud must have left Paris for Charleville about 25 March 1872.

4. The date of Rimbaud's return to Paris is as uncertain as the date oɪ his departure to Charleville a few weeks earlier (see note 3 above). There is a letter from Rimbaud to Delahaye dated 'Parmerde, juinphe, 1872' which is presumably 'Paris, juin, 1872', in the course of which he refers to the room he had rented in Paris in the Rue Monsieur-le-Prince 'le mois passé' (i.e. May 1872). There is also a letter from Verlaine to Rimbaud dated simply 'mai 1872' discussing the question of the latter's return the following Saturday and referring to 'tes trois mois d'Ardennes'. Verlaine is certainly exaggerating if Rimbaud only left Paris on 25 March, as suggested in note 3 above, but he was no doubt thinking of the three months March, April, and May rather than the actual length of Rimbaud's absence. It seems likely, however, that it was towards the end rather than towards the beginning of May that Rimbaud returned to Paris.

5. The legendary islands of the Hesperides lie to the west away from the morning sun; could Rimbaud be using a periphrasis to describe the moon which figures later in the poem?

6. Perhaps 'de mousse' may be an adjectival expression meaning 'moss-green'; seen through the leaves of trees in spring an empty construction site might not unreasonably be called a 'moss-green desert'.

7. See A. Adam, *O.C. 1972*, p. 932, note 1.

8. See Margaret Davies, 'Bonne Penseé du matin', *French Studies*, 1971, p. 295.

9. On the manuscript of his poem, written in prison in 1874, Verlaine

noted that it was: 'A propos d'une chambre, rue Campagne-Première, à Paris, en janvier 1872'.

10. This letter can be found in Verlaine's *Oeuvres complètes*, Paris, Club du meilleur livre, 1959, 1, 976, and in Ex-Mme. Paul Verlaine, *Mémoires de ma vie*, Flammarion, 1935, p, 219.

11. Antoine Adam repeats Suzanne Bernard's error of describing an 'almée' as a 'danseuse des Indes' although the word is in fact Arabic in origin and is defined in the *Petit Robert* as a 'danseuse égyptienne'.

12. Pierre Petitfils believes that the original manuscript was photographed and that it was on the photograph that the date August 1872 was added, and the initials A.R., although the handwriting may well not be Rimbaud's. See Pierre Petitfils in the magazine *Le Bateau ivre*, July 1962.

13. Various corrections were made on the photograph of the manuscript referred to in the preceding note, one of which was the substitution of 'les charbons' for 'les Terres'. The word 'goût' on the other hand is underlined on the original manuscript. For further details on this matter see Antoine Adam's note, in *O.C. 1972*, p. 939, on Pierre Petitfils' article referred to in note 12 above.

14. See C. A. Hackett, 'Verlaine's influence on Rimbaud', in *Studies in Modern French Literature*, edited by L. J. Austin, Garnet Rees and Eugène Vinaver, Manchester University Press, 1961, pp. 163–180.

15. Although the content and the versification of 'Mémoire' may suggest that it is contemporary with 'Le Bateau ivre', it must be added that the style, particularly the changing and, in consequence, confusing imagery, suggests a somewhat later date. It may be that when Rimbaud returned to Charleville from Paris in the spring of 1872 he felt that the 'bateau ivre' had become once more a 'canot immobile' and that this explains the relationship between the two poems.

IV. THE *ILLUMINATIONS*: 1872–?

1. For further details see C. Chadwick, *Etudes sur Rimbaud*, pp. 78–9.

2. See V. P. Underwood, *Rimbaud et l'Angleterre*, pp. 328–9; N. Osmond (ed.) *Illuminations*, pp. 15–16 and p. 177, note 18; C. Chadwick *Etudes sur Rimbaud*, pp. 86–91.

3. See Antoine Adam, 'L'énigme des *Illuminations*', *Revue des Sciences Humaines*, 1950, and the notes on the *Illuminations* in *O.C. 1972*, pp. 972–1020.

4. See D. De Graaf, *Arthur Rimbaud, homme de lettres*, van Gorkum, Assen, 1948, and 'Les *Illuminations* et la date exacte de leur composition', *Revue des Sciences Humaines*, 1950.

5. See Suzanne Bernard, ed. cit., Introduction, pp. lix–lxii and notice, pp. 246–51.

6. See M. Ruff, *Rimbaud*, pp. 190–239.

7. See E. Starkie, *Arthur Rimbaud*, pp. 231–2.

8. See V. P. Underwood, op. cit. passim.

9. See N. Osmond, ed. cit., Introduction, p. 5.

10. See Arthur Rimbaud *Oeuvres complètes*, Gallimard, 1963, Avertissement, pp. xi–xii.

11. See *French Studies*, 1961, p. 275.

12. See C. Chadwick, *Etudes sur Rimbaud*, pp. 74–132.

13. See N. Osmond, ed. cit., Introduction, p. 12. See also note 56 below.

14. Ibid., p. 16.

15. 'Démocratie' may well have been inspired by a general disapproval, on Rimbaud's part, of the colonial expansion that was so marked a feature of the policy of western European countries in the nineteenth century. It may also have been more specifically inspired by some particular colonial episode, but the difficulty is to decide which one. A. Adam, of course, considers that 'Rimbaud évoque son passage dans la légion étrangère hollandaise à Java en 1876'; V. P. Underwood, on the other hand, emphasises that in 1874 Britain was engaged in a colonial war in Ashanti in West Africa (op. cit., p. 292); but he also acknowledges that this particular episode had filled the newspaper headlines from May 1873. No firm conclusion can therefore be drawn as to the date of 'Démocratie'.

16. See *O.C. 1972*, p. 987.

17. See N. Osmond, ed. cit., p. 173. It should be noted that Osmond and most other critics differ from Antoine Adam who scornfully dismisses the idea that there is an optimistic note in the final lines; he prefers to see the passage as a bitter admission by Rimbaud of the bankruptcy of his ideas: '"Solde" exprime avec une force bouleversante l'échec de la grande tentative de Rimbaud. Il liquide' (*O.C. 1972*, p. 1006).

18. See above, Chapter III, note 3.

19. V. P. Underwood, op. cit., p. 299, suggests that the couple in 'Royauté' may be Queen Victoria and Prince Albert. The relationship between the Prince and his Queen was, however, the reverse of the relationship between the dominant male figure and the trembling female figure in 'Royauté'.

20. The expression 'exquise mort' is used in 'Les Indolents' in Verlaine's *Fêtes galantes*.

21. Rimbaud gives the Scandinavian name of Henrika to one of the figures in 'Ouvriers' whom he further describes as wearing 'une jupe de coton à carreau blanc et brun, qui a dû être portée au siècle dernier, un bonnet à rubans et un foulard de soie'. Because of this wealth of detail Antoine Adam is inclined to date the passage from as late as 1877, when Rimbaud was in Sweden, and to see Henrika as a real female figure and not as a symbolic portrait of Verlaine.

22. Antoine Adam notes that the opening words seem to echo a line from one of the poems in Verlaine's *La Bonne Chanson*: 'Isolés dans l'amour

ainsi qu'en bois noir', and that the next few words are reminiscent of two lines from *Romances sans paroles:*

> Soyons deux enfants, soyons deux jeunes filles,
> Eprises de rien et de tout étonnées.

23. As the epigraph to 'Il pleure dans mon cœur' in *Romances sans paroles* Verlaine quotes a line from Rimbaud which does not in fact exist: 'Il pleut doucement sur la ville'. It seems possible that this may be a poorly remembered version of 'pleut doucement sur ma veillée'.

24. The expression 'fêtes de fraternité' would seem to suggest the French 'fête nationale' of 14 July. On 14 July 1872 Rimbaud was somewhere in northern France or southern Belgium, having left Paris with Verlaine on 7 July. On 14 July 1873 he was in hospital in Brussels recovering from the gunshot wound inflicted by Verlaine on 10 July. On 14 July 1874 he was in London. 14 July 1872 would therefore seem to be the most likely date for this particular text, thus supporting the view that the passages of 'Phrases' as a whole are concerned with the relationship with Verlaine. It should, however, be added that M. Ruff, op. cit., pp. 204–5, denies that the fall of the Bastille was celebrated on a national scale until after 1880 and contends that Rimbaud's 'fêtes de fraternité' refer simply to 'quelque fête communale populaire, qui a pu se dérouler à n'importe quelle date, dans n'importe quel pays'.

25. N. Osmond, ed. cit., p. 135.

26. Strictly speaking it is the word 'charrue', not the word 'char', which means 'plough'; but in view of the phrase 'soulèvent les souches des ronces' Rimbaud must be allowing himself some poetic licence here.

27. See Suzanne Bernard, ed. cit., pp. 510–11.

28. See *O.C. 1972*, pp. 999–1000.

29. See V. P. Underwood, op. cit., Illustrations 7, 8 and 55, for photographs of these houses showing the basements. Underwood makes the further suggestion (pp. 309–10) that Rimbaud may be referring to the Tower Subway beneath the Thames, but the second paragraph seems to argue against this.

30. See ibid. Illustrations 11 and 11 *bis* for examples of such lampposts.

31. N. Osmond, ed. cit., p. 147.

32. See *O.C. 1972*, pp. 995–6.

33. See V. P. Underwood, op. cit., pp. 341–3.

34. Ibid., pp. 174–93.

35. N. Osmond, ed. cit., p. 146.

36. See V. P. Underwood, op. cit., pp. 288–9.

37. V. P. Underwood, op. cit., reproduces an illustration (No. 33) by Gustave Doré of Ludgate Circus, published in 1872 in W. B. Jerrold's *London*. Such inextricable traffic jams seem perhaps a more likely source for the second paragraph of 'Métropolitain' than the more static scene by Doré (illustration No. 37) that Underwood also suggests as a source.

Illustrations Nos. 30 and 47 in *Rimbaud et l'Angleterre* are also the kind of scene that may have inspired Rimbaud's metaphor.

38. It should be noted that the relative simplicity of 'Aube' and its similarities with the phrases quoted from Rimbaud's letter to Delahaye written in Paris in June 1872 suggest that it too may date from about that time. But the presence of the German word 'wasserfall' has inclined some critics to date the passage from the weeks Rimbaud spent in Stuttgart in 1875, even though he left Germany for Italy before the summer of that year.

39. Beneath the imagery of these lines it seems possible to perceive much the same idea as in the preliminary 'lettre du voyant' to Izambard dated 13 May 1871: 'Les souffrances sont énormes, mais il faut être fort, être né poète, et je me suis reconnu poète'.

40. Towards the end of 'Délires I' in *Une Saison en enfer* the 'époux infernal' addresses the 'vierge folle' as 'chère âme', echoing the 'cher corps' and 'cher cœur' of 'Enfance I', although it is, of course, possible that Rimbaud may be expressing the tedium of physical relationships in general and not just of one specific relationship.

41. See Verlaine's letter to Lepelletier of 26 December 1872 in his *Correspondance*, i, p. 80, and in *Oeuvres complètes*, Club du meilleur livre, i, p. 1017.

42. See *O.C. 1972*, pp. 1016–17; N. Osmond, ed. cit., pp. 157–9; V. P. Underwood, op. cit., pp. 310–15; C. Chadwick, *Etudes sur Rimbaud*, pp. 118–19; Albert Py (ed.), *Illuminations*, pp. 220–1; M. Davies, 'Rimbaud and Melville', *Revue de littérature comparée*, 1969, pp. 479–89.

43. See *O.C. 1972*, p. 980.

44. Rimbaud's juxtaposition of 'démon' and 'dieu' shortly after his mention of 'amour' is reminiscent of Verlaine's words in the first version of 'Crimen Amoris': 'Il faut l'Amour, meure Dieu, meure le Diable'.

45. See N. Osmond, ed. cit., pp. 143–4.

46. See *O.C. 1972*, pp. 1004–5.

47. See Henri de Bouillane de Lacoste, *Rimbaud et le problème des Illuminations*, Mercure de France, 1949, p. 227.

48. See *O.C. 1972*, p. 985.

49. See, for example, N. Osmond, ed. cit., pp. 104–5; Albert Py (ed.), *Illuminations*, p. 105.

50. See N. Osmond, ed. cit., p. 173.

51. These elements of versification in 'Veillées I', 'Départ', 'Marine' and 'Mouvement' could be taken as further evidence for dating these poems from 1872, in addition to the evidence offered by their content in the case of three of them.

52. V. P. Underwood would no doubt dispute that this is an image and that it has any of the connotations suggested – see note 19 above.

53. See W. M. Frohock, *Rimbaud's Poetic Practice*, pp. 162–170 for an analysis of this aspect of Rimbaud's style.

54. In only one case does Rimbaud write on both sides of the paper, 'Nocturne vulgaire' being on one side of a sheet and the two short passages 'Marine' and 'Fête d'hiver' being on the other.

55. There are only about a dozen instances of Rimbaud substituting one word for another or inserting a word in a line already written. It is to be noted, however, that these occasional corrections and insertions are, on the whole, clumsily done, which would suggest that Rimbaud was not preparing a fair copy for the printer as some critics believe. It should also be noted that although three quarters of the passages are on the same kind of paper, the handwriting varies quite considerably. This too strongly suggests that the *Illuminations* were not copied out all at once but were written over a considerable period of time.

56. It should be noted that if the manuscript of the *Illuminations* is both a first and a final version, this could support at least part of N. Osmond's thesis, namely that where two passages share the same sheet, or where passages flow over from one sheet to the next, then they are in the order in which Rimbaud originally wrote them. Thus it could be argued that 'Antique' must have been written just before 'Being Beauteous' since the two passages occupy the upper and lower halves of the same sheet of paper; and that 'Vies', 'Départ' and 'Royauté' must have been written in that order since 'Départ' is in the middle of a sheet bearing the end of 'Vies' and the beginning of 'Royauté'. There are eight other groupings of this kind – 'Enfance' and 'Conte'; 'A une raison', 'Matinée d'ivresse' and 'Phrases'; 'Ouvriers', 'Les Ponts', 'Ville' and 'Ornières'; 'Villes I', 'Vagabonds' and 'Villes II'; 'Veillées', 'Mystique', 'Aube' and 'Fleurs'; 'Marine' and 'Fête d'hiver' (with 'Nocturne vulgaire' on the other side of the same sheet); 'Angoisse', 'Métropolitain' and 'Barbare'; and finally 'Bottom' and 'H'.

On the other hand, it could equally well be argued that Rimbaud copied out the passages in random order, sticking rigorously to his principles as a 'voyant' and refusing to correct even the most obvious and superficial mistakes in his original versions.

V. *UNE SAISON EN ENFER*: 1873

1. A more detailed account of the events surrounding the publication of *Une Saison en enfer* can conveniently be found in the 1954 edition of the *Oeuvres complètes*. The *O.C. 1972* edition gives a much briefer account.

2. Vitalie Rimbaud notes in her diary her brother's arrival at Roche on Good Friday 11 April 1873 (see *O.C. 1972* p. 819); it should be noted that on p. 817 this section of Vitalie's diary is wrongly headed 'août 1874' when it should read 'avril-septembre 1873'.

3. It is interesting to note that Verlaine too seems to have regarded April 1873 as marking a distinct break in his life and work. Hence the fact that *Romances sans paroles* has no poems in it dating from after April

and that *Sagesse* has several poems in it written between April and July. So that although, with the benefit of hindsight, July 1873 now appears to mark the end of the Verlaine-Rimbaud relationship, it seems clear that they themselves thought that this particular chapter in their lives was finished in April and that they did not, at that time, expect to come together again for a final few weeks from 24 May to 20 July. For further details on this point see C. Chadwick, *Verlaine* (Athlone French Poets), The Athlone Press, University of London, 1973, pp. 51–3.

4. The incorrect spellings are, of course, deliberate and form part of the adolescent style that Rimbaud adopted in his letters at this time.

5. See N. Osmond, ed. cit., Introduction, p. 7.

6. In 1968 M. Ruff in his *Rimbaud*, pp. 173–5, revived a suggestion made by R. Clauzel in 1931 that the 'vierge folle' and 'l'époux infernal' were not Verlaine and Rimbaud but were two aspects of the latter's character. Antoine Adam, in *O.C. 1972*, p. 962, gives the suggestion his approval, but few, if any, other critics regard it as tenable.

7. M. Ruff puzzles over why the words 'l'époux infernal' are in smaller lettering than the words 'vierge folle' and are placed below rather than beside the latter. The reason may be to indicate that they do not form part of the sub-title of the passage but are used, as in a play, to designate the person who speaks the first line and, indirectly, the whole passage.

8. 'Pourquoi souligner *"moi, la pauvre âme"* ', asks M. Ruff, op. cit., p. 174. The most likely explanation is that these words are quoted from an earlier poem by Rimbaud, 'Chanson de la plus haute tour', in which, with reference to Verlaine, he had talked of the 'mille veuvages de la si pauvre âme', the notion of 'veuvage' also being repeated in 'Délires I'.

9. For further discussion of this point see C. Chadwick, *Verlaine*, p. 42 and *Etudes sur Rimbaud*, p. 50.

10. See Suzanne Bernard, ed. cit., p. 473, note 29.

11. See C. Chadwick, *Verlaine*, pp. 68–9.

12. It is interesting to note that, at about the same time, Verlaine gave a similar significance to autumn in the final line of his sonnet 'L'espoir luit . . .' (see Paul Verlaine, *Sagesse*, edited by C. Chadwick (Athlone French Poets), The Athlone Press, University of London, 1973, pp. 91–3).

13. These 'nouvelles fleurs' seem to echo the 'fleurs de rêve' of Enfance I and the 'fleurs magiques' of 'Enfance II', as well as the exotic flowers of the passage 'Fleurs'. The 'nouveaux astres' may well refer to the 'lunes et comètes' and the 'boules de saphir, de métal' that Rimbaud imagines in the centre of the earth in 'Enfance V'. The 'nouvelles chairs' seem to be an apt description of the fantasy creatures of 'Antique' and 'Being Beauteous'.

14. C. A. Hackett reaches a similar conclusion in *Une Saison en enfer: frénésie et structure*: 'Ainsi, *Une Saison en enfer*, malgré la frénésie présente dans les conflits qui s'y trouvent retracés, nous apparaît comme une

construction très concertée et même un peu trop linéaire. Au lieu de créer et de suggérer comme dans les *Illuminations*, Rimbaud raconte, affirme, explique. Cette œuvre est bien, comme il l'a écrit lui-même, la "relation" de son enfer' (*La Revue des Lettres Modernes*, Nos. 370–3, 1973, pp. 7–15).

SELECT BIBLIOGRAPHY

EDITIONS

Rimbaud, *Oeuvres complètes*, edited by Antoine Adam, Gallimard, Bibliothèque de la Pléiade, 1972. (N.B. This edition has superseded the earlier Pléiade edition prepared by Rolland de Renéville and Jules Mouquet in 1946 and revised in 1954.)

Rimbaud, *Oeuvres*, edited by Suzanne Bernard, Garnier, 1960.

Rimbaud, *Illuminations*, edited by N. Osmond (Athlone French Poets), The Athlone Press, University of London, 1976.

CRITICISM

Y. Bonnefoy, *Rimbaud par lui-même*, Editions du Seuil, 1961.

C. Chadwick, *Etudes sur Rimbaud*, Nizet, 1960.

M. Eigeldinger, *La voyance avant Rimbaud*, Droz & Minard, 1975.

R. Etiemble, *Le Mythe de Rimbaud*, vol. 1 *La Genèse du mythe*, vol. 2 *La Structure du mythe*, Gallimard 1952.

W. M. Frohock, *Rimbaud's Poetic Practice*, Oxford University Press, 1963.

C. A. Hackett, *Rimbaud l'enfant*, Corti, 1948

—, *Rimbaud*, Bowes and Bowes, 1957

—, *Autour de Rimbaud*, Klincksieck, 1967.

J. P. Houston, *The Design of Rimbaud's poetry*, Yale University Press, 1963.

H. Matarasso and P. Petitfils, *Vie de Rimbaud*, Hachette, 1962

—, *Album Rimbaud*, Gallimard, Bibliothèque de la Pléiade, 1967.

E. Noulet, *Le Premier visage de Rimbaud*, Brussels, Palais des Académies, 1953.

P. Petitfils, *L'œuvre et le visage de Rimbaud*, Nizet, 1949.

A. R. de Renéville, *Rimbaud le voyant*, La Colombe, 1946.

M. Ruff, *Rimbaud*, Hatier, 1968.

E. Starkie, *Arthur Rimbaud*, Faber and Faber, 1961.

V. P. Underwood, *Rimbaud et l'Angleterre*, Nizet, 1976.

INDEX

Athlone French Poets

General Editor EILEEN LE BRETON
*Reader in French Language and Literature,
Bedford College, University of London*

Monographs

GERARD DE NERVAL
THEOPHILE GAUTIER
VERLAINE
RIMBAUD
JULES LAFORGUE
PAUL VALERY
GUILLAUME APOLLINAIRE
SAINT-JOHN PERSE
HENRI MICHAUX

Critical Editions

VICTOR HUGO : CHATIMENTS
GERARD DE NERVAL : LES CHIMERES
ALFRED DE MUSSET : CONTES D'ESPAGNE ET D'ITALIE
THEOPHILE GAUTIER : POESIES
PAUL VERLAINE : SAGESSE
PAUL VERLAINE : ROMANCES SANS PAROLES
ARTHUR RIMBAUD : LES ILLUMINATIONS
JULES LAFORGUE : LES COMPLAINTES
PAUL VALERY : CHARMES OU POEMES
GUILLAUME APOLLINAIRE : ALCOOLS
SAINT-JOHN PERSE : EXIL
MICHAUX : AU PAYS DE LA MAGIE